LIFE OF
MICHELANGELO
BUONARROTI

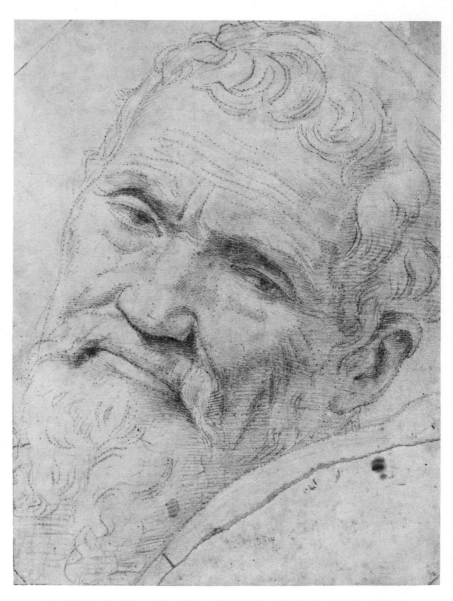

MICHELANGELO IN OLD AGE BY DANIELE DA VOLTERRA
Black chalk, pricked for transfer. *Teyler Museum, Haarlem.*

Giorgio Vasari

LIFE OF MICHELANGELO BUONARROTI

TRANSLATED
WITH AN INTRODUCTION BY
GEORGE BULL
AND MICHELANGELO WORKS
SELECTED BY
PETER MURRAY

The Folio Society

LONDON MCMLXXI

PRINTED IN GREAT BRITAIN

Printed and bound by W & J Mackay & Co Ltd, Chatham
Set in Bembo 13 point leaded 1 point
Illustrations lithographed by Westerham Press Ltd, Westerham

Contents

Introduction

IN THE second edition of the *Lives of the Most Excellent Sculptors, Painters and Architects,* which was seen through the press in Florence in 1568, Giorgio Vasari informed his fellow artists that of the large number of volumes printed of the first edition, eighteen years before, not one had been left on the booksellers' hands. A best seller when they were first published four hundred years ago, his biographies of the artists of the Renaissance have over the centuries maintained both their wide popular appeal and their immense historical value.

Vasari was born in 1511 (about the time Henry VIII came to the throne of England) in Arezzo, a Tuscan town which was subject to the Republic of Florence. He was a year old when by force of Spanish arms the Medici family were restored to power in Florence (to rule there almost without interruption for over two hundred years). As he grew up the dynastic conflict between France and Spain, in which Florence became a pawn in the Spanish camp, was caught up in the shattering turmoil of the Reformation. When he died in his early sixties the Catholic world was busy on harsh internal reform and offensive military action against Protestant states and rulers. The city state of Florence had long since settled down to the paternal rule of a Medici duke. Still developing vigorously in the north of Europe, in Italy the ideas and attitudes of the Renaissance were being modified or reversed.

Though a fairly pious Catholic and a fierce patriot, Vasari was not the slightest bit interested in the religious and political issues of his time: the faintest whiff of gunpowder or heresy was enough to send him running for cover. Like Uccello, murmuring about the beauties of perspective as his wife nagged him to come to bed, like his contemporary Benvenuto Cellini, a braver but not a better man, Vasari was obsessed by art: the pictures and plans he was pouring out himself, the products and performance of his fellow artists. Nevertheless, the *Lives* were shaped by the historical circumstances of sixteenth-century Italy: autocratic governments in Rome and

Florence, a balance between freedom of movement and incipient censorship of thought, and a newly established role for the artist in society, partly servant to the court and the people and partly a professional answerable to himself and God alone.

At the end of the *Lives* Vasari included a 'Description' of his own works. From this and from what he tells us elsewhere emerges an autobiography which is valuable chiefly for the light it throws on the genesis of the *Lives*.

He came of a family of tradesmen (the name Vasari derives from *vasaro* or *vasaio*, a potter) which had already given one famous name to art, that of Luca Signorelli, the cousin of Giorgio's grandfather who gave Giorgio some of his first lessons in drawing. His father, Antonio Vasari, was none too well off (Giorgio was the eldest son of a very big family) but tolerably well connected. He encouraged Giorgio's talent for drawing (as a child Giorgio copied 'all the good pictures to be found in the churches of Arezzo'); then in 1524 he used a family connexion to give the boy his big chance, taking him along to pay his respects to Cardinal Silvio Passerini, who was passing through Arezzo on his way, as representative of the newly elected Medici Pope, Clement VII, to take over the government of Florence during the minority of Alessandro and Ippolito de' Medici.

'When he saw that the boy, who was no more than nine [*sic*] years old . . . had been so well taught that he knew by heart a great part of Virgil's Aeneid, which he had him recite, and heard that he had been taught how to draw by the French painter Guglielmo da Massiglia, he told Antonio to bring him to Florence.'

Vasari recounts that the cardinal put him to study with Michelangelo in Florence, but almost immediately Michelangelo was called to Rome and he was placed with Andrea del Sarto instead. One would like to know more about the first, providential encounter between the middle-aged Michelangelo and the young Vasari. For over the years Michelangelo came increasingly to value and encourage Giorgio's enthusiastic friendship and Vasari came to idolize Michelangelo as an artist and to revere him as a man; the scheme and structure of the *Lives*, published a quarter of a century after they first met, depend completely on the climax provided by the *Life* of Michelangelo.

After a good start, with Andrea del Sarto and Baccio Bandinelli as his teachers, Vasari's first few years as a practising artist were fairly harassed and precarious. His father died of the plague, leaving him a family to support; Florence – in revolt against the Medici in 1527 and besieged in 1529 – was for some years a centre of unrest and war. A busy and fruitful interlude was cut short in 1537, when his patron, Duke Alessandro, was assassinated. This was a crushing blow to Vasari's hopes and self-esteem.

'I found myself' (he wrote later) 'robbed of all the expectations held out by his favour . . . and I determined no longer to seek my fortune at court but to follow art alone, though I could easily have had a position with the new duke, Cosimo de' Medici.'

Vasari's immediate reaction to the death of Alessandro was to become ill: he had a nervous breakdown. After he recovered, for four years he refused to return to Florence. During this period, however, and after he again set up house in Florence in 1540, he worked busily, wandering from town to town as far south as Naples, covering canvases and walls with pictures for a variety of patrons and, more fortunately for posterity, filling his notebooks with sketches of the works he saw on his travels. The idea of writing the *Lives* took shape.

By now, in his thirties, Vasari was a highly successful painter, his services constantly in demand and well paid for, the employer of a band of assistants and a propertied man with influential friends, of considerable standing among his fellow artists. He was argued into marriage by one of his friends and patrons, Cardinal del Monte (the future Julius III). The *Lives* were published and acclaimed.

At length, in 1555, he returned to serve the Medici rulers of Florence, appointed by Duke Cosimo as architect for the Palazzo Vecchio and sacrificing his freedom for erratic but powerful patronage and the status of official artist and impresario. He corresponded on terms of growing familiarity with Michelangelo, founded in Florence in 1563 the first of the new academies of art – the *Accademia del Disegno* – which exactly institutionalized the professional and academic purposes of the artists of the time, and arranged elaborate ceremonies and decorative schemes for the ruling family. In preparation for the second edition of the *Lives* he went on a grand tour of Italian towns, checking his facts, gathering new material and consulting with friends. When the revised and far bulkier edition was published, at fifty-seven, he was the respected doyen of the art world of Rome and Tuscany.

The remaining six years of his life were spent in a glow of self-satisfaction and public recognition (his work for Pope Pius V won him a knighthood in 1571), punctuated by worries about his health and his salary and by tiffs with other artists, but otherwise happily devoted to vast and uninspired decorative projects in Rome and Florence, including notably the decoration of the dome of Santa Maria del Fiore. He and Grand Duke Cosimo – grown very fond of each other – died in the same year, 1574, ten years after the death of Michelangelo.

From his earliest years Vasari was a keen collector of the drawings of the great masters and of stories about them. Of the drawings, Vasari made his *Libro di disegni*, to which he refers very often in the *Lives*. The fabulous collection no longer exists, though many of the items are extant. He tells in his own biography how the idea of a great history of the artists was finally formed.

When in 1546 he was decorating the Cancelleria in Rome for Cardinal Farnese he used to go along in the evenings and join the cardinal while he was having supper and enjoying the conversation of various artists and writers such as the poet Francesco Maria Molza, Annibale Caro, translator and littérateur, and Paolo Giovio, the biographer and art collector. On one of those evenings

the conversation turned to Giovio's museum and the portraits of famous men that he has collected . . . Giovio said that he had always wanted and would still like to have as well as his museum and his book of eulogies a treatise discussing all illustrious artists from the time of Cimabue up to the present. Enlarging on this, he showed that he enjoyed considerable judgement and understanding in regard to the arts. But it must be said that, talking in general terms, he was careless about details and often made up stories about the artists. . . . When Giovio had finished this discourse the cardinal turned to me and said:

'What do you say, Giorgio? Would this not be a fine work?'

'Splendid,' I answered, 'if Giovio were to be helped by someone of the profession to put things in the right places and to describe matters as they really were. I'm saying this because although what he told us was admirable he had changed and confused many things.'

This I readily promised to do, as best I could, though I knew it was really beyond my powers. And so I started to look through my memoranda and notes, which I had been gathering on this subject since my childhood as a pastime and because of the affection I bore towards the memory of our artists, every scrap of information about whom was precious to me. Then I put together everything that seemed relevant and took the material along to Giovio. . . .

Giovio, adds Vasari, persuaded him to undertake the complete work himself. And he agreed to this, intending, however, to publish it under a name other than his own.

Some doubts have been cast on the reliability of Vasari's account of the famous dinner-party at Cardinal Farnese's when the subject of the *Lives* was broached. By then, he was already collecting his material. The substantial accuracy of his account, however, is accepted. In gathering his material, checking his facts, writing and revising the *Lives*, Vasari was heavily dependent on the help and ideas of others. He leaned, above all, for literary advice on his friend ('they're really one, though they seem two', said Cellini) the Florentine prior, Vincenzo Borghini. He pressed into his service all kinds of sources, occasionally to the point of plagiarism: traditions handed down by word of mouth, the recollection of his own friends and correspondents and the considerable body of written material already in existence (the *Commentaries* of Ghiberti, for example, the anonymous Life of Brunelleschi, Boccaccio's *Decameron* and many other biographies, chronicles, commentaries, and records).

The theories of the nature and history of art which are expressed in and through the *Lives* were similarly derivative. Vasari's achievement was to fuse in a work of great literary merit all the knowledge possessed by Florentine artists about their incomparable artistic heritage and the art theories current in intellectual circles in Florence and Rome. In doing this, he also achieved an impressive success as a critic.

He wrote, above all, for his fellow artists, and his purpose was essentially to establish and maintain artistic standards. The complete text of the *Lives*, indeed, includes Vasari's '*parte teorica*' or three-part Introduction, dealing in a highly technical and practical fashion with the methods and materials of architecture, sculpture, and painting.

I have endeavoured (he claimed in his preface to the second part of the *Lives*) to distinguish between the good, the better, and the best. . . . I have tried as well as I know how to help people who cannot find out for themselves how to understand the sources and origins of various styles. . . .

The acceptance of rise and decline in the affairs of men and the idea that a rebirth or renaissance of the fine arts had taken place in Tuscany were both common currency in the intellectual world of Vasari's time. For the idea of a rebirth of the arts, however, Vasari gave compelling chapter and verse: the signs were first seen in such and such buildings, such and such works of sculpture; the men who some two hundred years before had first turned away from the degenerate art of the post-classical world were Cimabue and Giotto, legendary figures to some extent, but artists many of whose works could still be seen and whose influence could be traced on succeeding generations. In the second period flourished the flesh-and-blood figures of Ghiberti, Brunelleschi, and Donatello; in the third, when the arts reached the 'summit of perfection', men who worked within living memory or were still alive, Leonardo and Raphael and Michelangelo.

'The man whose work transcends and eclipses that of every other artist,' wrote Vasari, 'is the inspired Michelangelo Buonarroti, who is supreme not in one art alone but in all three. He surpasses not only all those whose work can be said to be superior to nature but also the artists of the ancient world, whose superiority is beyond doubt. Michelangelo has triumphed over later artists, over the artists of the ancient world, over nature itself, which has produced nothing, however challenging or extraordinary, that his inspired genius, with its great powers of application, design, artistry, judgement, and grace, has not been able to surpass with ease. He has shown his genius not only in painting and colouring but also in the creation of sculptural works in full relief. And his fruitful and inspiring labours have already spread their branches so wide that the world has been filled with an abundance of delectable fruits, and the three fine arts have been brought to a state of complete perfection. He has so enhanced the art of sculpture that we can say without fear of contradiction that his statues are in every aspect far superior to those of the ancient world. For if their work were put side by side, the heads, hands, arms, and feet carved by Michelangelo being compared with those made by the ancients, his would be seen to be fashioned on sounder principles and executed with more grace and perfection: the effortless intensity of his graceful style defies comparison. And the same holds true of Michelangelo's pictures: if it were possible to place them beside the paintings of those celebrated Greeks and Romans they would be even more highly valued and regarded as being as much superior to the antiques as is his sculpture.'

In their entirety, the *Lives* may fairly be called a work of art. On one great canvas Vasari painted a harmonious and glowing composition which sustains with ease the task of conveying the revolutionary nature of what happened in Italian art between the fourteenth and sixteenth centuries. He lifted the story of Tuscan art – a series of explosive discoveries by men chosen by God – to the plane of the heroic, stretching back to the quasi-legendary figures of Cimabue and Giotto, and forward to the inspired Michelangelo Buonarroti, genius and saint.

We are well informed on the works of Michelangelo since Vasari wrote his first *Life* before 1550, while Michelangelo was still alive. In 1553 Michelangelo's pupil, Ascanio Condivi, wrote an authorized biography intended to correct those parts of Vasari's *Life* which Michelangelo himself did not like. These two, together with the final version of Vasari's *Life*, written after Michelangelo's death in 1564, give a very complete account of all his major works. In particular, they record the three great fresco cycles in the Vatican and the cartoon for a fresco in Florence, which was destroyed early in the sixteenth century but is known to us in part from Michelangelo's preparatory drawings and from an early partial copy now in the collection of the Earl of Leicester.

The *Life* of Michelangelo (as expanded in the second edition of Vasari's *Lives* to become the fullest account yet published of an artist's career) clearly and boldly reflects the almost mystical reverence in which Michelangelo was held, after the painting of the Sistine Chapel, as the greatest living artist. Happily, Vasari's fondness for anecdote, for anxiety to show

how well he knew the inspired Buonarroti, and his curious eye for colourful and amusing incident make the *Life* a fascinating narrative not only of Michelangelo's high claims and almost superhuman achievements but also of his marvellous humanity, in its frustrations, affections and eccentricities.

GEORGE BULL

Life of
Michelangelo Buonarroti

Florentine painter, sculptor, and architect

1475–1564

ENLIGHTENED BY what had been achieved by the renowned
Giotto and his school, all artists of energy and distinction were
striving to give the world proof of the talents with which
fortune and their own happy temperaments had endowed them.
They were all anxious (though their efforts were in vain) to reflect
in their work the glories of nature and to attain, as far as possible,
perfect artistic discernment or understanding. Meanwhile, the benign
ruler of heaven graciously looked down to earth, saw the worthless-
ness of what was being done, the intense but utterly fruitless studies,
and the presumption of men who were farther from true art than
night is from day, and resolved to save us from our errors. So he
decided to send into the world an artist who would be skilled in each
and every craft, whose work alone would teach us how to attain
perfection in design (by correct drawing and by the use of contour
and light and shadows, so as to obtain relief in painting) and how to
use right judgement in sculpture and, in architecture, create buildings
which would be comfortable and secure, healthy, pleasant to look at,
well-proportioned, and richly ornamented. Moreover, he determined to give this artist the knowledge of true moral philosophy
and the gift of poetic expression, so that everyone might admire and
follow him as the perfect exemplar in life, work, and behaviour, and
in every endeavour, and he would be acclaimed as divine. He also
saw that in the practice of these exalted disciplines and arts, namely,
painting, sculpture, and architecture, the Tuscan genius has always

been pre-eminent, for the Tuscans have devoted to all the various branches of art more labour and study than all the other Italian peoples. And therefore he chose to have Michelangelo born a Florentine, so that one of her own citizens might bring to absolute perfection the achievements for which Florence was already justly renowned.

So in the year 1474 in the Casentino, under a fateful and lucky star, the virtuous and noble wife of Lodovico di Leonardo Buonarroti gave birth to a baby son. That year Lodovico (who was said to be related to the most noble and ancient family of the counts of Canossa) was visiting magistrate at the township of Chiusi and Caprese near the Sasso della Vernia (where St Francis received the stigmata) in the diocese of Arezzo. The boy was born on Sunday, 6 March, about the eighth hour of the night; and without further thought his father decided to call him Michelangelo, being inspired by heaven and convinced that he saw in him something supernatural and beyond human experience. This was evident in the child's horoscope which showed Mercury and Venus in the house of Jupiter, peaceably disposed; in other words, his mind and hands were destined to fashion sublime and magnificent works of art. Now when he had served his term of office Lodovico returned to Florence and settled in the village of Settignano, three miles from the city, where he had a family farm. That part of the country is very rich in stone, especially in quarries of greystone which are continuously worked by stone-cutters and sculptors, mostly local people; and Michelangelo was put out to nurse with the wife of one of the stone-cutters. That is why once, when he was talking to Vasari, he said jokingly:

'Giorgio, if my brains are any good at all it's because I was born in the pure air of your Arezzo countryside, just as with my mother's milk I sucked in the hammer and chisels I use for my statues.'

As time passed and Lodovico's family grew bigger he found himself, as he enjoyed only a modest income, in very difficult circumstances and he had to place his sons in turn with the Wool and Silk Guilds. When Michelangelo was old enough he was sent to the grammar school to be taught by Francesco of Urbino; but he was so obsessed by drawing that he used to spend on it all the time he possibly could. As a result he used to be scolded and sometimes beaten by his father and the older members of the family, who most likely considered it unworthy of their ancient house for Michelangelo to give his time to an art that meant nothing to them. It was about this time that Michelangelo became friendly with the young Francesco Granacci, who had been sent as a boy to learn the art of painting from Domenico Ghirlandaio.* Francesco saw that Michelangelo had a great aptitude for drawing, and as he was very fond of him he used to supply him every day with drawings by Ghirlandaio, who was then regarded, throughout all Italy let alone in Florence, as one of the finest living masters. As a result Michelangelo grew more ambitious with every day that passed, and when Lodovico realized that there was no hope of forcing him to give up drawing he resolved to put his son's aspirations to some use and make it possible for him to learn the art properly. So on the advice of friends he apprenticed him to Domenico Ghirlandaio.

When this happened Michelangelo was fourteen years old. And incidentally, the author of a biography of Michelangelo which was written after 1550 (when I wrote these *Lives* the first time) says that some people, because they did not know Michelangelo personally, have said things about him that were never true and have left out others that deserved to be mentioned.† For instance, he himself taxes Domenico with envy and alleges that he never gave any help to Michelangelo. But this accusation is plainly false, as can be judged from something written by Michelangelo's father, Lodovico, in one

* Domenico Ghirlandaio (1449–94), a competent painter, chiefly in fresco, who ran a large family studio in Florence.
† Ascanio Condivi, Michelangelo's pupil, whose *Life of Michelangelo*, closely supervised by Michelangelo himself, was published in 1553.

of Domenico's record books, which is now in the possession of his heirs. The entry reads as follows:

1488. This first day of April I record that I, Lodovico di Leonardo Buonarroti, do apprentice my son Michelangelo to Domenico and David di Tommaso di Currado for the next three years, under the following conditions: that the said Michelangelo must stay for the stipulated time with the above-named to learn and practise the art of painting, and that he should obey their orders, and that the same Domenico and David should pay him in those three years twenty-four florins of full weight: six in the first year, eight in the second year. and ten in the third year, to a total of ninety-six lire.

And below this, also in Lodovico's handwriting, is the following entry or record:

The above-named Michelangelo received this sixteenth day of April two gold florins, and I, Lodovico di Leonardo, his father, received twelve lire and twelve soldi on his account.

I have copied these entries straight from the book in order to show that everything I wrote earlier and am writing now is the truth; nor am I aware that anyone was more familiar with Michelangelo than I or can claim to have been a closer friend or more faithful servant, as can be proved to anyone's satisfaction. Moreover, I do not believe there is anyone who can produce more affectionate or a greater number of letters than those written by Michelangelo and addressed to me. I made this digression for the sake of truth, and it must suffice for the rest of his *Life*. And now let us go back to Michelangelo himself.

The way Michelangelo's talents and character developed astonished Domenico, who saw him doing things quite out of the ordinary for boys of his age and not only surpassing his many other pupils but also very often rivalling the achievements of the master himself. On one occasion it happened that one of the young men studying with Domenico copied in ink some draped figures of women from Domenico's own work. Michelangelo took what he had drawn and, using a thicker pen, he went over the contours of one of the figures and brought it to perfection; and it is marvellous to see the difference between the two styles and the superior skill and judgement of a young man so spirited and confident that he had the courage to correct what his teacher had done. This drawing is now kept by me among my treasured possessions. I received it from Granacci, along with other drawings by Michelangelo, for my book of drawings; and in 1550, when he was in Rome, Giorgio Vasari showed it to Michelangelo who recognised it and was delighted to see it again. He said modestly that as a boy he had known how to draw better than he did now as an old man.

Another time, when Domenico was working on the principal chapel of Santa Maria Novella, Michelangelo came along and started to draw the scaffolding and trestles and various implements and materials, as well as some of the young men who were busy there. When Domenico came back and saw what Michelangelo had done he said: 'This boy knows more about it than I do.' And he stood there astonished at the originality and skill in imitation that his inborn sense of judgement enabled so young an artist to display. Certainly, the work showed all the qualities to be expected of an artist with years of experience. This was because the instinctive grace of Michelangelo's work was enhanced by study and practice; and every day he produced work that was still more inspired. For example, it was at that time that he made the copy of an engraving by Martin the German that brought him considerable fame.* Michelangelo did a perfect pen-and-ink copy of this copper engraving, which showed St Anthony being tormented by devils, soon after it had been brought to Florence. He also did the scene in colours; and for this purpose in order to copy some of the strange-looking demons in the picture he went along to

* Martin Schongauer (1453–91), a painter and engraver of Colmar.

the market and bought some fishes with fantastic scales like theirs. The skill with which he did this work won him a considerable reputation. Michelangelo also copied the works of other masters, with complete fidelity; he used to tinge his copies and make them appear black with age by various means, including the use of smoke, so that they could not be told apart from the originals. He did this so that he could exchange his copies for the originals, which he admired for their excellence and which he tried to surpass in his own works; and these experiments also won him fame.

At that time the custodian or keeper of all the fine antiques that Lorenzo the Magnificent had collected at great expense and kept in his garden on the Piazza di San Marco was the sculptor Bertoldo.* He had been a pupil of Donatello's, and the chief reason why Lorenzo kept him in his service was because he had set his heart on establishing a school of first-rate painters and sculptors and wanted Bertoldo to teach and look after them. Bertoldo was now too old to work; nevertheless, he was very experienced and very famous, not only for having polished the bronze pulpits cast by Donatello but also for the many bronze casts of battle-scenes and the other small things he had executed himself with a competence that no one else in Florence could rival. So Lorenzo, who was an enthusiastic lover of painting and sculpture, regretting that he could find no great and noble sculptors to compare with the many contemporary painters of ability and repute, determined, as I said, to found a school himself. For this reason he told Domenico Ghirlandaio that if he had in his workshop any young men who were drawn to sculpture he should send them along to his garden, where they would be trained and formed in a manner that would do honour to himself, to Domenico, and to the whole city. So Domenico gave him some of the best among his young men, including Michelangelo and Francesco Granacci. And when they arrived at the garden they found Torrigiano (a young man of the Torrigiani family) working there on some clay figures in the

* Giovanni di Bertoldo (c. 1420–91).

round that Bertoldo had given him to do.* After he had seen these figures, Michelangelo was prompted to make some himself; and when he saw the boy's ambitious nature Lorenzo started to have very high hopes of what he would do. Michelangelo was so encouraged that some days later he set himself to copy in marble an antique faun's head which he found in the garden; it was very old and wrinkled, with the nose damaged and a laughing mouth. Although this was the first time he had ever touched a chisel or worked in marble, Michelangelo succeeded in copying it so well that Lorenzo was flabbergasted. Then, when he saw that Michelangelo had departed a little from the model and followed his own fancy in hollowing out a mouth for the faun and giving it a tongue and all its teeth, Lorenzo laughed in his usual charming way and said:

'But you should have known that old folk never have all their teeth and there are always some missing.'

In his simplicity Michelangelo, who loved and feared that lord, reflected that this was true, and as soon as Lorenzo had gone he broke one of the faun's teeth and dug into the gum so that it looked as if the tooth had fallen out; then he waited anxiously for Lorenzo to come back. And after he had seen the result of Michelangelo's simplicity and skill, Lorenzo laughed at the incident more than once and used to tell it for a marvel to his friends. He resolved that he would help and favour the young Michelangelo; and first he sent for his father, Lodovico, and asked whether he could have the boy, adding that he wanted to keep him as one of his own sons. Lodovico willingly agreed, and then Lorenzo arranged to have Michelangelo given a room of his own and looked after as one of the Medici household. Michelangelo always ate at Lorenzo's table with the sons of the family and other distinguished and noble persons who lived with that lord, and Lorenzo always treated him with great respect. All this happened the year after Michelangelo had been placed with Domenico, when

* Pietro Torrigiano (1472–1528), a Florentine sculptor who worked in England. notably on the tomb of Henry VII.

he was fifteen or sixteen years old; and he lived in the Medici house for four years, until the death of Lorenzo the Magnificent in 1492. During that period, as salary and so that he could help his father, Michelangelo was paid five ducats a month; and to make him happy Lorenzo gave him a violet cloak and appointed his father to a post in the Customs. As a matter of fact all the young men in the garden were paid salaries varying in amount through the generosity of that noble and magnificent citizen who supported them as long as he lived. It was at this time that, with advice from Politian, a distinguished man of letters, Michelangelo carved from a piece of marble given him by Lorenzo the Battle of Hercules with the Centaurs. This was so beautiful that today, to those who study it, it sometimes seems to be the work not of a young man but of a great master with a wealth of study and experience behind him. It is now kept in memory of Michelangelo by his nephew Lionardo, who cherishes it as a rare work of art. Not many years ago Lionardo also kept in his house in memory of his uncle a marble Madonna in bas-relief, little more than two feet in height. This was executed by Michelangelo when he was still a young man after the style of Donatello, and he acquitted himself so well that it seems to be by Donatello himself, save that it possesses more grace and design. Lionardo subsequently gave this work to Duke Cosimo de' Medici, who regards it as unique, since it is the only sculpture in bas-relief left by Michelangelo.

To return to the garden of Lorenzo the Magnificent: this place was full of antiques and richly furnished with excellent pictures collected for their beauty, and for study and pleasure. Michelangelo always held the keys to the garden as he was far more earnest than the others and always alert, bold, and resolute in everything he did. For example, he spent many months in the church of the Carmine making drawings from the pictures by Masaccio; he copied these with such judgement that the craftsmen and all the others who saw his work were astonished, and he then started to experience envy as well as fame.

It is said that Torrigiano, who had struck up a friendship with Michelangelo, then became jealous on seeing him more honoured than himself and more able in his work. At length Torrigiano started to mock him, and then he hit him on the nose so hard that he broke and crushed it and marked Michelangelo for life. Because of this, Torrigiano, as I describe elsewhere, was banished from Florence.

When Lorenzo the Magnificent died, Michelangelo went back to live with his father, filled with sorrow at the death of a great man who had befriended every kind of talent. While he was with his father he obtained a large block of marble from which he carved a Hercules eight feet high, which stood for many years in the Palazzo Strozzi. This work, which was very highly regarded, was later (when Florence was under siege) sent to King Francis in France by Giovan-battista della Palla. It is said that Piero de' Medici, who had been left heir to his father, Lorenzo, often used to send for Michelangelo, with whom he had been intimate for many years, when he wanted to buy antiques such as cameos and other engraved stones. And one winter, when a great deal of snow fell in Florence, he had him make in his courtyard a statue of snow, which was very beautiful. Piero did Michelangelo many favours on account of his talents, and Michel-angelo's father, seeing his son so highly regarded among the great, began to provide him with far finer clothes than he used to.

For the church of Santo Spirito in Florence Michelangelo made a crucifix of wood which was placed above the lunette of the high altar, where it still is. He made this to please the prior, who placed some rooms at his disposal where Michelangelo very often used to flay dead bodies in order to discover the secrets of anatomy; and in this way he started to perfect the great powers of design that he sub-sequently enjoyed.

It happened that a few weeks before the Medici were driven out of Florence Michelangelo had left for Bologna and then gone on to Venice, since he feared, when he saw the insolence and bad government of Piero de' Medici, that because of his connexion with the Medici family he would run into trouble himself. Being unable to find any means of living in Venice, he went back to Bologna. But thoughtlessly he failed to find out when he entered through the gate the password for going out again. (As a precaution, Giovanni Bentivogli had ordered that foreigners who could not give the password should pay a penalty of fifty Bolognese lire.) Now when he found himself in this predicament, without the money to pay the fine, by chance Michelangelo was seen by Giovanfrancesco Aldovrandi, one of the Sixteen of the Government, who felt sorry for him, and after he had heard his story secured his release and then gave him hospitality in his own home for more than a year. One day Aldovrandi took Michelangelo to see the tomb of St Dominic which had been executed (as I describe elsewhere) by the early sculptors, Giovanni Pisano and, later, Niccolò dell'Arca. There were two figures missing: an angel holding a candelabrum and a St Petronius, both about two feet high. Aldovrandi asked Michelangelo if he had the courage to do them, and he answered yes. So he had the marble given to Michelangelo, who executed the two figures, which proved to be the finest on the tomb. Aldovrandi paid him thirty ducats for this work.

Michelangelo stayed in Bologna just over a year, and he would have stayed longer in order to repay Aldovrandi for his kindness. (Aldovrandi loved him for his skill as an artist and also because of his Tuscan accent, which he enjoyed when Michelangelo read him work by Dante, Petrarch, Boccaccio, and other poets.) However, as he realized that he was wasting time, Michelangelo was only too happy to return to Florence. And there, for Lorenzo di Pierfrancesco de' Medici, he made a little St John in marble, and then immediately started work on another marble figure, a sleeping Cupid, life-size. When this was finished, Baldassare del Milanese showed it as a beautiful piece of work to Lorenzo di Pierfrancesco, who agreed with his judgement and said to Michelangelo:

'If you were to bury it and treat it to make it seem old and then send it to Rome, I'm sure that it would pass as an antique and you would get far more for it than you would here.'

Michelangelo is supposed to have then treated the statue so that it looked like an antique; and this is not to be marvelled at seeing that he was ingenious enough to do anything. Others insist that Milanese took it to Rome and buried it in a vineyard he owned and then sold it as an antique for two hundred ducats to Cardinal San Giorgio. Others again say that Milanese sold the cardinal the statue that Michelangelo had made for him, and then wrote to Pierfrancesco saying that he should pay Michelangelo thirty crowns since that was all he had got for the Cupid; and in this way he deceived the cardinal, Lorenzo di Pierfrancesco, and Michelangelo himself. But then afterwards, the cardinal learned from an eye-witness that the Cupid had been made in Florence, discovered the truth of the matter through a messenger, and compelled Milanese's agent to restore his money and take back the Cupid. The statue later came into the possession of Duke Valentino who presented it to the marchioness of Mantua; and she took it back to her own part of the world where it is still to be seen today. Cardinal San Giorgio did not escape censure for what happened, since he failed to recognize the obviously perfect quality of Michelangelo's work. The fact is that, other things being equal, modern works of art are just as fine as antiques; and there is no greater vanity than to value things for what they are called rather than for what they are. However, every age produces the kind of man who pays more attention to appearances than to facts.

All the same this work did so much for Michelangelo's reputation that he was immediately summoned to Rome to enter the service of Cardinal San Giorgio, with whom he stayed nearly a year, although the cardinal, not understanding the fine arts very much, gave him nothing to do.* At that time the cardinal's barber, who had been a

* Michelangelo went to Rome first in 1496. The Popes he served were Julius II (1503–13), Leo X (1513–21), Clement VII (1523–34), Paul III (1534–49), Julius III (1550–5), Paul IV (1555–9), and Pius IV (1559–65).

painter and worked very studiously in tempera, though he had no draughtsmanship, struck up a friendship with Michelangelo, who drew for him a cartoon showing St Francis receiving the stigmata; and this was very carefully painted by the barber on a panel which is to be found in the first chapel on the left, as one enters the church of San Pietro in Montorio. Michelangelo's abilities were then clearly recognized by a Roman gentleman called Jacopo Galli, and this discerning person commissioned from him a marble life-size statue of Cupid and then a Bacchus, ten spans high, holding a cup in his right hand and the skin of a tiger in his left, with a bunch of grapes which a little satyr is trying to nibble. In this figure it is clear that Michelangelo wanted to obtain a marvellous harmony of various elements, notably in giving it the slenderness of a youth combined with the fullness and roundness of the female form. This splendid achievement showed that Michelangelo could surpass every other sculptor of the modern age. Through the studies he undertook while in Rome he acquired such great skill that he was able to solve incredibly difficult problems and to express in a style of effortless facility the most elevated concepts, to the sheer amazement not only of those who lacked the experience to judge but also of men accustomed to excellent work. All the other works then being created were regarded as trivial compared with what Michelangelo was producing. As a result the French cardinal of Saint-Denis, called Cardinal Rouen,★ became anxious to employ his rare talents to leave some suitable memorial of himself in the great city of Rome; and so he commissioned Michelangelo to make a Pietà of marble in the round, and this was placed, after it was finished, in the chapel of the Madonna della Febbre in St Peter's, where the temple of Mars once stood. It would be impossible for any craftsman or sculptor no matter how brilliant ever to surpass the grace or design of this work or try to cut and polish the marble with the skill that Michelangelo displayed. For the Pietà was a revelation

★ This was Jean Villier de la Grolaie, abbot of Saint-Denis and cardinal of Santa Sabina.

of all the potentialities and force of the art of sculpture. Among the many beautiful features (including the inspired draperies) this is notably demonstrated by the body of Christ itself. It would be impossible to find a body showing greater mastery of art and possessing more beautiful members, or a nude with more detail in the muscles, veins, and nerves stretched over their framework of bones, or a more deathly corpse. The lovely expression of the head, the harmony in the joints and attachments of the arms, legs, and trunk, and the fine tracery of pulses and veins are all so wonderful that it staggers belief that the hand of an artist could have executed this inspired and admirable work so perfectly and in so short a time. It is certainly a miracle that a formless block of stone could ever have been reduced to a perfection that nature is scarcely able to create in the flesh. Michelangelo put into this work so much love and effort that (something he never did again) he left his name written across the sash over Our Lady's breast. The reason for this was that one day he went along to where the statue was and found a crowd of strangers from Lombardy singing its praises; then one of them asked another who had made it, only to be told: 'Our Gobbo from Milan.'*

Michelangelo stood there not saying a word, but thinking it very odd to have all his efforts attributed to someone else. Then one night, taking his chisels, he shut himself in with a light and carved his name on the statue. And a fine poet has aptly described the Pietà, which is full of truth and life, as follows:

> Bellezza ed onestate,
>   E doglia, e pieta in vivo marmo morte,
>   Deh, come voi pur fate,
>   Non piangete sí forte,
>   Che anzi tempo risveglisi da morte.
>   E pur, mal grado suo,
>   Nostro Signore, e tuo

* Cristoforo Solari.

Sposo, figliuolo e padre,
*Unica sposa sua figliuola e madre.**

This work did wonders for Michelangelo's reputation. To be sure, there are some critics, more or less fools, who say that he made Our Lady look too young. They fail to see that those who keep their virginity unspotted stay for a long time fresh and youthful, just as those afflicted as Christ was do the opposite. Anyhow, this work added more glory and lustre to Michelangelo's genius than anything he had done before.

Then some of his friends wrote to him from Florence urging him to return there as it seemed very probable that he would be able to obtain the block of marble that was standing in the Office of Works. Piero Soderini, who about that time was elected Gonfalonier for life,† had often talked of handing it over to Leonardo da Vinci, but he was then arranging to give it to Andrea Contucci of Monte Sansovino, an accomplished sculptor who was very keen to have it. Now, although it seemed impossible to carve from the block a complete figure (and only Michelangelo was bold enough to try this without adding fresh pieces) Buonarroti had felt the desire to work on it many years before; and he tried to obtain it when he came back to Florence. The marble was eighteen feet high, but unfortunately an artist called Simone da Fiesole had started to carve a giant figure, and had bungled the work so badly that he had hacked a hole between the legs and left the block completely botched and misshapen. So the wardens of Santa Maria del Fiore (who were in charge of the undertaking) threw the block aside and it stayed abandoned for many years and seemed

* The verse was by Giovan Battista Strozzi il Vecchio, poet and madrigalist, and is very obscure. Roughly and literally: 'Beauty and goodness, And grief and pity, alive in the dead marble, Do not, as you do, weep so loudly, Lest before time should awake from death, In spite of himself, Our Lord, and thy Spouse, son and father, Oh virgin, only spouse, daughter and mother.'
† Soderini was elected *Gonfaloniere di Justizia* for life (in effect, head of the Florentine Republic) in 1502.

likely to remain so indefinitely. However, Michelangelo measured it again and calculated whether he could carve a satisfactory figure from the block by accommodating its attitude to the shape of the stone. Then he made up his mind to ask for it. Soderini and the wardens decided that they would let him have it, as being something of little value, and telling themselves that since the stone was of no use to their building, either botched as it was or broken up, whatever Michelangelo made would be worthwhile. So Michelangelo made a wax model of the young David with a sling in his hand; this was intended as a symbol of liberty for the Palace, signifying that just as David had protected his people and governed them justly, so whoever ruled Florence should vigorously defend the city and govern it with justice. He began work on the statue in the Office of Works of Santa Maria del Fiore, erecting a partition of planks and trestles around the marble; and working on it continuously he brought it to perfect completion, without letting anyone see it.

As I said, the marble had been flawed and distorted by Simone, and in some places Michelangelo could not work it as he wanted; so he allowed some of the original chisel marks made by Simone to remain on the edges of the marble, and these can still be seen today. And without any doubt, Michelangelo worked a miracle in restoring to life something that had been left for dead.

After the statue had been finished, its great size provoked endless disputes over the best way to transport it to the Piazza della Signoria. However, Giuliano da Sangallo, with his brother Antonio, constructed a very strong wooden framework and suspended the statue from it with ropes so that when moved it would sway gently without being broken; then they drew it along by means of winches over planks laid on the ground, and put it in place. In the rope which held the figure suspended he tied a slip-knot which tightened as the weight increased: a beautiful and ingenious arrangement. (I have a drawing by his own hand in my book showing this admirable, strong, and secure device for suspending weights.)

When he saw the David in place Piero Soderini was delighted; but while Michelangelo was retouching it he remarked that he thought the nose was too thick. Michelangelo, noticing that the Gonfalonier was standing beneath the Giant and that from where he was he could not see the figure properly, to satisfy him climbed on the scaffolding by the shoulders, seized hold of a chisel in his left hand, together with some of the marble dust lying on the planks, and as he tapped lightly with the chisel let the dust fall little by little, without altering anything. Then he looked down at the Gonfalonier, who had stopped to watch, and said:

'Now look at it.'

'Ah, that's much better,' replied Soderini. 'Now you've really brought it to life.'

And then Michelangelo climbed down, feeling sorry for those critics who talk nonsense in the hope of appearing well informed. When the work was finally finished he uncovered it for everyone to see. And without any doubt this figure has put in the shade every other statue, ancient or modern, Greek or Roman. Neither the Marforio in Rome, nor the Tiber and the Nile of the Belvedere, nor the colossal statues of Monte Cavallo can be compared with Michelangelo's David, such were the satisfying proportions and beauty of the finished work. The legs are skilfully outlined, the slender flanks are beautifully shaped and the limbs are joined faultlessly to the trunk. The grace of this figure and the serenity of its pose have never been surpassed, nor have the feet, the hands, and the head, whose harmonious proportions and loveliness are in keeping with the rest. To be sure, anyone who has seen Michelangelo's David has no need to see anything else by any other sculptor, living or dead.

The David (for which Piero Soderini paid Michelangelo four hundred crowns) was put in position in the year 1504. It established Michelangelo's reputation as a sculptor and he went on to make for the Gonfalonier a very fine David in bronze, which Soderini sent to France. At this time Michelangelo also blocked out (without ever finishing) two marble roundels, one for Taddeo Taddei (which is to be found in his house today) and the other for Bartolommeo Pitti (and this was given by Fra Miniato Pitti of Monte Oliveto, a great student of cosmography and other subjects, especially painting, to his dear friend Luigi Guicciardini). These works were highly admired and appreciated. In addition, Michelangelo blocked out in the Office of Works of Santa Maria del Fiore a marble statue of St Matthew. Rough as it is, this is a perfect work of art which serves to teach other sculptors how to carve a statue out of marble without making any mistakes, perfecting the figure gradually by removing the stone judiciously and being able to alter what has been done as and when necessary.

Michelangelo also made a bronze tondo of Our Lady which he cast at the request of certain Flemish merchants of the Mouscron family, men of great distinction in their own country, who paid him a hundred crowns and sent the work to Bruges. Then Angelo Doni, a Florentine who loved to own beautiful things by ancient or modern artists, decided he would like his friend to make something for him. So Michelangelo started work on a round painting of the Madonna. This picture shows Our Lady kneeling down and holding out the child to St Joseph. The mother of Christ turns her head and gazes intently on the supreme beauty of her son with an air of marvellous contentment lovingly shared with the venerable St Joseph, who takes the child with similar affection, tenderness, and reverence, as we can see from a glance at his face. Not content with this achievement, to show his superb mastery of painting, Michelangelo depicted in the background several nude figures, some leaning, others standing and seated. He executed this work with such care and diligence that it is held beyond doubt as the most beautiful and perfect of the few panel pictures he painted. When it was ready he sent it under wrappings to Angelo's house with a note asking for payment of seventy ducats. Now Angelo, who was careful with his money, was disconcerted at being asked to spend so much on a picture, even though he knew

31

that, in fact, it was worth even more. So he gave the messenger forty ducats and told him that that was enough. Whereupon Michelangelo returned the money with a message to say that Angelo should send back either a hundred ducats or the picture itself. Then Angelo, who liked the painting, said: 'Well, I'll give him seventy.'

However, Michelangelo was still far from satisfied. Indeed, because of Angelo's breach of faith he demanded double what he had asked first of all, and this meant that to get the picture Angelo was having to pay a hundred and forty ducats.

It happened that while the great painter Leonardo da Vinci was working in the Council Chamber (as I related in his biography) Piero Soderini, who was then Gonfalonier, recognizing Michelangelo's abilities, had part of the hall allocated to him; and this was why Michelangelo painted the other wall in competition with Leonardo, taking as his subject an episode in the Pisan War. For this project Michelangelo used a room in the Dyers' Hospital at Sant'Onofrio, where he started work on a vast cartoon which he refused to let anyone see. He filled it with naked men who are bathing because of the heat in the River Arno when suddenly upon an attack by the enemy the alarm is raised in the camp. And as the soldiers rush out of the water to dress themselves Michelangelo's inspired hand depicted some hurrying to arm themselves in order to bring help to their comrades, others buckling on their cuirasses, many fastening other pieces of armour on their bodies, and countless more dashing into the fray on horseback. Among the rest was the figure of an old man wearing a garland of ivy to shade his head; he is sitting down to pull on his stockings, but he cannot do so because his legs are wet from the water, and as he hears the cries and tumult of the soldiers and the beating of the drums he is straining to draw on one stocking by force. The nerves and muscles of his face and his contorted mouth convey the frenzied effort and exertion he is making with his whole body. There were some drummers and other naked figures, with their clothes bundled up, hurrying to get to the fighting, and drawn in various unusual attitudes: some upright, some kneeling or leaning forward, or half-way between one position and another, all exhibiting the most difficult foreshortenings. There were also many groups of figures drawn in different ways: some outlined in charcoal, others sketched with a few strokes, some shaded gradually and heightened with lead-white. This Michelangelo did to show how much he knew about his craft. When they saw the cartoon, all the other artists were overcome with admiration and astonishment, for it was a revelation of the perfection that the art of painting could reach. People who have seen these inspired figures declare that they have never been surpassed by Michelangelo himself or by anyone else, and that no one can ever again reach such sublime heights. And this may readily be believed, for after the cartoon had been finished and, to the glory of Michel-angelo, carried to the Sala del Papa, with tremendous acclamations from all the artists, those who subsequently studied it and made copies of the figures (as was done for many years in Florence by local artists and others) became excellent painters themselves. As we know, the artists who studied the cartoon included Aristotile de Sangallo (Michelangelo's friend), Ridolfo Ghirlandaio, Raphael Sanzio of Urbino, Francesco Granacci, Baccio Bandinelli, and the Spaniard Alonso Beruguete. They were followed by Andrea del Sarto, Francia-bigio, Jacopo Sansovino, Rosso, Maturino, Lorenzetto, and Tribolo, when he was a child, and by Jacopo da Pontormo and Perin del Vaga. All these men were outstanding Florentine artists.

The cartoon having thus become a school for craftsmen, it was taken to the great upper room of the house of the Medici. But this meant that it was unwisely left in the hands of the craftsmen; and when Duke Giuliano fell ill, without warning it was torn into pieces. And now it is dispersed in various places. For example, there are some fragments still to be seen at Mantua in the house of Uberto Strozzi, a Mantuan gentleman, who preserves them with great rever-ence; and certainly anyone who sees them is inclined to think them of divine rather than human origin.

Michelangelo had become so famous because of his Pietà, the colossal statue of David at Florence, and the cartoon, that when in 1503 Alexander VI died and Julius II was elected Pope (at which time Buonarroti was about twenty-nine years old) Julius very graciously summoned him to Rome to build his tomb; and to meet the expenses of the journey he was paid a hundred crowns by the Pope's agent. After he had arrived in Rome, however, many months were let go by before he was asked to do any work. But eventually the Pope chose for his tomb the design made by Michelangelo. This design was an eloquent proof of Michelangelo's genius, for in beauty and magnificence, wealth of ornamentation and richness of statuary it surpassed every ancient or imperial tomb ever made. When he saw it Pope Julius grew more ambitious and resolved to set about rebuilding the church of St Peter's at Rome, and to raise his tomb inside.

So Michelangelo started work with very high hopes, going first of all with two of his assistants to Carrara to excavate all the marble, on account of which he received a thousand crowns from Alamanni Salviati in Florence. He had nothing more by way of money or supplies for the eight months he spent in the mountains, where inspired by the masses of stone he conceived many fantastic ideas for carving giant statues in the quarries, in order to leave there a memorial of himself, as the ancients had done. After he had chosen all the marble that was wanted he had it loaded on board ship and taken to Rome, where the blocks filled half the square of St Peter's around Santa Caterina and between the church and the corridor leading to Castel Sant'Angelo. In the castle Michelangelo had prepared his room for executing the figures and the rest of the tomb; and so that he could come and see him at work without any bother the Pope had ordered a drawbridge to be built from the corridor to the room. This led to great intimacy between them, although in time the favours he was shown brought Michelangelo considerable annoyance and even persecution, and stirred up much envy among his fellow craftsmen.

Of this work Michelangelo executed during the lifetime and after the death of Julius four statues completed, and eight which were only blocked out, as I shall describe. Since the design of the tomb illustrates Michelangelo's extraordinary powers of invention, we shall describe here the plan that he followed. To give a sense of grandeur he intended the tomb to be free-standing so as to be seen from all four sides. The sides measured twenty-four feet in one direction and thirty-six in the other, the dimensions therefore being a square and a half. All round the outer side of the tomb were a range of niches, divided one from the other by terminal figures (clothed from the middle upwards) which supported the first cornice with their heads; and each of these figures had fettered to it, in a strange and curious attitude, a nude captive standing on a projection of the base. These captives were meant to represent all the provinces subjugated by the Pope and made obedient to the Apostolic Church; and there were various other statues, also fettered, of all the liberal arts and sciences, which were thus shown to be subject to death no less than the pontiff himself, who employed them so honourably. On the corners of the first cornice were to go four large figures, representing the Active and the Contemplative Life, St Paul, and Moses. The tomb rose above the cornice in gradually diminishing steps, with a decorated bronze frieze, and with other figures, *putti*, and ornaments all around; and at the summit, completing the structure, were two figures, one of which was Heaven, smiling and supporting a bier on her shoulder, and the other, Cybele, the goddess of the Earth, who appeared to be grief-stricken at having to remain in a world robbed of all virtue through the death of such a great man, in contrast to Heaven who is shown rejoicing that his soul had passed to celestial glory. The tomb was arranged so that one might enter and come out between the niches at the ends of the quadrangle; and the interior was in the shape of an oval, curving like a temple. The sarcophagus to take the Pope's dead body was to go in the middle. Finally, the tomb was to have forty marble statues, not to mention the other scenes, *putti*, and ornamentation, and the richly carved cornices and other architectural elements.

To hurry the work on, Michelangelo arranged that some of the marble should be taken to Florence, where he intended at times to pass the summer in order to avoid the malaria of Rome; and there he executed one side of the work in several sections down to the last detail. With his own hand he finished in Rome two of the captives, which were truly inspired, and other statues which have never been surpassed. As they were never used for the tomb, these captives were given by Michelangelo to Roberto Strozzi, when he happened to be lying ill in his house. Subsequently they were sent as a gift to King Francis, and they are now at Ecouen in France. In Rome he also blocked out eight statues, and in Florence another five, along with a Victory surmounting the figures of a captive, which are now in the possession of Duke Cosimo, to whom they were given by Michelangelo's nephew, Lionardo. His excellency has put the Victory in the Great Hall of his palace, which was painted by Vasari. Michelangelo also finished the Moses, a beautiful statue in marble ten feet high. With this no other modern work will ever bear comparison (nor, indeed, do the statues of the ancient world). For, seated in an attitude of great dignity, Moses rests one arm on the tablets that he is grasping in one hand, while with the other he is holding his beard, which falls in long ringlets and is carved in the marble so finely that the hairs (extremely difficult for the sculptor to represent) are downy and soft and so detailed that it seems that Michelangelo must have exchanged his chisel for a brush. Moreover, the face of Moses is strikingly handsome, and he wears a saintly and regal expression; indeed, one cries out for his countenance to be veiled, so dazzling and resplendent does it appear and so perfectly has Michelangelo expressed in the marble the divinity that God first infused in Moses' most holy form. In addition, the draperies worn by Moses are carved and finished with beautiful folds in the skirt; and the arms with their muscles and the hands with their bones and tendons are so supremely beautiful, the legs, knees, and feet are covered with such carefully fashioned hose and sandals, and every part of the work is finished so expertly, that today more than ever Moses can truly be called the friend of God. For, through the skill of Michelangelo, God has wanted to restore and prepare the body of Moses for the Resurrection before that of anyone else. And well may the Jews continue to go there (as they do every Sabbath, both men and women, like flocks of starlings) to visit and adore the statue, since they will be adoring something that is divine rather than human.

Eventually everything was agreed and the work approached completion; and subsequently, of the four, one of the shorter sides was erected in San Pietro in Vincoli. It is said that while Michelangelo was working on the tomb, the marbles which had remained at Carrara were brought to the Ripa Grande port at Rome and then conveyed to St Peter's square to join the rest. As those who had brought them had to be paid Michelangelo went (as he usually did) to see the Pope. But because that day his holiness was transacting some important business concerning Bologna, Michelangelo returned home and paid for the marble himself, thinking that he would straight away be repaid by his holiness. Then he went back another time to talk to the Pope about it, but he found difficulty in getting in for one of the grooms told him that he would have to be patient and that he received orders not to admit him. At this a bishop who happened to be there said to the groom: 'You can't know who this man is.'

'I know him only too well,' replied the groom. 'But it's my job to do what I'm told to by my superiors and by the Pope.'

This attitude incensed Michelangelo, who had never experienced such treatment before, and he angrily told the groom that he should let his holiness know that if ever he wanted to see him in future he would find he had gone elsewhere. Then he went back to his workplace, and at the second hour of the night he set out on post-horses, leaving two servants to sell everything in the house to the Jews and then follow him to Florence. After he had arrived at Poggibonzi, in the territory of Florence, Michelangelo felt safe; but shortly afterwards five couriers arrived with instructions from the Pope to bring him back. For all their entreaties, and despite the letter which ordered him to return to Rome under threat of punishment, he refused to listen to a word. Eventually, however, the couriers persuaded him to write a word or two in answer to his holiness, in which he asked to be forgiven but added that he would never again return to his presence, since he had had him driven off like a criminal, that his faithful service had not deserved such treatment, and that the Pope should look for someone else to serve him.

Having arrived at Florence, Michelangelo devoted himself during the three months he stayed there to finishing the cartoon for the Great Hall, which Piero Soderini wanted him to carry into execution. However, during that time three papal briefs arrived at the Signoria commanding that Michelangelo be sent back to Rome; and when he saw the Pope's vehemence, as he distrusted him, Michelangelo contemplated, so it is said, going off to Constantinople to serve the Grand Turk, who was anxious to secure his services (through the agency of certain Franciscans) to build a bridge from Constantinople to Pera. However, against his will he was persuaded by Piero Soderini to go and meet the Pope as a public servant of Florence, protected by the title of ambassador. Finally, the Gonfalonier recommended him to his brother, Cardinal Soderini, for presentation to the Pope and sent him to Bologna, where his holiness had already arrived from Rome.

(Another explanation is given for Michelangelo's flight from Rome: namely, that the Pope became angry with him because he would not allow any of his work to be seen; that Michelangelo distrusted his own men and suspected that the Pope, as did in fact happen more than once, disguised himself to see what was being done when he was away himself; and that on one of these occasions the Pope bribed his assistants to let him in to see the chapel of his uncle Sixtus, which as I describe later he was having painted by Michelangelo, only for Michelangelo, who had suspected this treachery and hidden himself, to hurl planks at him when he came in, without considering who it might be, and make him retreat in a fury. Anyhow, whatever happened, one way or another he quarrelled with the Pope and then grew afraid and had to run away.)

Michelangelo arrived at Bologna, where no sooner had he taken off his riding-boots than he was escorted by the Pope's servants to his holiness who was in the Palace of the Sixteen. As Cardinal Soderini was ill he sent one of his bishops to accompany him, and when they arrived in front of the Pope and Michelangelo knelt down, his holiness looked at him askance as if he were angry and said:

'So instead of your coming to meet us you have waited for us to meet you?' (By this he meant that Bologna was nearer to Florence than to Rome.)

With a courteous gesture, and speaking in a firm voice, Michelangelo humbly begged the Pope's forgiveness, saying to excuse himself that he had acted as he did in anger, not having been able to bear being dismissed like that, but that if he had done wrong his holiness should forgive him once more. Then the bishop who had presented Michelangelo to the Pope began to make excuses for him, saying to his holiness that such men were ignorant creatures, worthless except for their art, and that he should freely pardon him. The Pope lost his temper at this and whacked the bishop with a crozier he was holding, shouting at him: 'It's you that are ignorant, insulting him in a way we wouldn't dream of.'

Then, when the groom had driven the bishop out with his fists, the Pope, having exhausted his anger, gave Michelangelo his blessing. And Michelangelo was detained in Bologna with gifts and promises, until his holiness ordered him to make a bronze figure of himself, ten feet high. In this statue of Julius, Michelangelo produced a beautiful work of art, expressing in its attitude both grandeur and majesty, adding rich and magnificent draperies, and in the countenance displaying courage, resolution, alertness, and an awesome dignity. When ready, the statue was placed in a niche over the door of San Petronio.

It is said that while Michelangelo was working on it he was visited by an accomplished goldsmith and painter called Francia who wanted to see what he was doing, as he had heard so much praise of Buonarroti and his works but had never seen any of them. Francia was given permission to inspect the statue, and the necessary arrangements were made. When at last he saw Michelangelo's artistry at first hand he was truly astonished. But then, on being asked what he thought of the figure, he remarked that it was a lovely casting, in a very fine material. Having heard Francia praise the statue for its bronze rather than its craftsmanship, Michelangelo said:

'Well, I owe as much to Pope Julius who gave me the bronze as you owe to the chemists who give you your colours for painting.'

Then, losing his temper, in the presence of all the gentlemen standing around he called Francia a fool. As part of the same story, when a son of Francia's was introduced to him as a very handsome young man Michelangelo said to him:

'The living figures your father makes are better than those he paints.'

Among the gentlemen present was one (I don't know his name) who asked Michelangelo what he thought was bigger, the statue of Julius or a pair of oxen. Michelangelo retorted:

'Well, it depends on the oxen. You see, an ox from Florence isn't as big as one from Bologna.'

Michelangelo finished the statue in clay before the Pope left Bologna for Rome, and so his holiness went to see it. The Pope did not know what was to be placed in the statue's left hand, and when he saw the right hand raised in an imperious gesture he asked whether it was meant to be giving a blessing or a curse. Michelangelo replied that the figure was admonishing the people of Bologna to behave sensibly. Then he asked the Pope whether he should place a book in the left hand, and to this his holiness replied:

'Put a sword there. I know nothing about reading.'

In the bank of Anton Maria da Lignano the Pope left a thousand crowns for the completion of the statue which was then, after Michelangelo had toiled on it for sixteen months, placed on the frontispiece in the main façade of San Petronio. (Later it was destroyed by the Bentivogli and the bronze was sold to Duke Alfonso of Ferrara, who used it to make a piece of artillery which was called *La Giulia*. All that was saved was the head, which is now in the duke's wardrobe.)

Meanwhile, the Pope had returned to Rome while Michelangelo remained in Bologna to finish the statue. In his absence Bramante was constantly plotting with Raphael of Urbino to remove from the Pope's mind the idea of having Michelangelo finish the tomb on his return. Bramante did this (being a friend and relation of Raphael and therefore no friend of Michelangelo's) when he saw the way his holiness kept praising and glorifying Michelangelo's work as a sculptor. He and Raphael suggested to Pope Julius that if the tomb were finished it would bring nearer the day of his death, and they said that it was bad luck to have one's tomb built while one was still alive. Eventually they persuaded his holiness to get Michelangelo on his return to paint, as a memorial for his uncle Sixtus, the ceiling of the chapel that he had built in the Vatican. In this way Bramante and Michelangelo's other rivals thought they would divert his energies from sculpture, in which they realized he was supreme. This, they argued, would make things hopeless for him, since as he had no experience of colouring in fresco he would certainly, they believed, do less creditable work as a painter. Without doubt, they thought, he would be compared unfavourably with Raphael, and even if the work were a success being forced to do it would make him angry with the Pope; and thus one way or another they would succeed in their purpose of getting rid of him. So when Michelangelo returned to Rome he found the Pope resolved to leave the tomb as it was for the time being, and he was told to paint the ceiling of the chapel. Michelangelo, being anxious to finish the tomb, and considering the magnitude and difficulty of the task of painting the chapel, and his

41

lack of experience, tried in every possible way to shake the burden off his shoulders. But the more he refused, the more determined he made the Pope, who was a wilful man by nature and who in any case was again being prompted by Michelangelo's rivals, and especially Bramante. And finally, being the hot-tempered man he was, his holiness was all ready to fly into a rage.

However, seeing that his holiness was persevering, Michelangelo resigned himself to doing what he was asked. Then the Pope ordered Bramante to make the ceiling ready for painting, and he did so by piercing the surface and supporting the scaffolding by ropes. When Michelangelo saw this he asked Bramante what he should do, when the painting was finished, to fill up the holes. Bramante said: 'We'll think of it when it's time.' And he added that there was no other way. Michelangelo realized that Bramante either knew nothing about the matter or else was no friend of his, and he went to the Pope and told him that the scaffolding was unsatisfactory and that Bramante had not known how to make it; and the Pope replied, in the presence of Bramante, that Michelangelo should do it himself in his own way. So he arranged to have the scaffolding erected on props which kept clear of the wall, a method for use with vaults (by which many fine works have been executed) which he subsequently taught to various people, including Bramante. In this instance he enabled a poor carpenter, who rebuilt the scaffolding, to dispense with so many of the ropes that when Michelangelo gave him what was over he sold them and made enough for a dowry for his daughter.

Michelangelo then started making the cartoons for the vaulting; and the Pope also decided that the walls that had been painted by previous artists in the time of Sixtus should be scraped clean and that Michelangelo should have fifteen thousand ducats for the cost of the work, the price being decided through Giuliano da Sangallo. Then being forced reluctantly, by the magnitude of the task, to take on some assistants, Michelangelo sent for help to Florence. He was anxious to show that his paintings would surpass the work done there earlier, and he was determined to show modern artists how to draw and paint. Indeed, the circumstances of this undertaking encouraged Michelangelo to aim very high, for the sake both of his own reputation and the art of painting; and in this mood he started and finished the cartoons. He was then ready to begin the frescoes, but he lacked the necessary experience. Meanwhile, some of his friends, who were painters, came to Rome from Florence in order to assist him and let him see their technique. Several of them were skilled painters in fresco and they included Granaccio, Giuliano Bugiardini, Jacopo di Sandro, the elder Indaco, Angelo di Donnino, and Aristotile. Having started the work, Michelangelo asked them to produce some examples of what they could do. But when he saw that these were nothing like what he wanted he grew dissatisfied, and then one morning he made up his mind to scrap everything they had done. He shut himself up in the chapel, refused to let them in again, and would never let them see him even when he was at home. So, when they thought the joke was wearing thin, they accepted their dismissal and went back ashamed to Florence.

Thereupon, having arranged to do all the work by himself, Michelangelo carried it well on the way to completion; working with the utmost solicitude, labour, and study he refused to let anyone see him in case he would have to show what he was painting. As a result every day the people became more impatient.

Pope Julius himself was always keen to see whatever Michelangelo was doing, and so naturally he was more anxious than ever to see what was being hidden from him. So one day he resolved to go and see the work, but he was not allowed in, as Michelangelo would never have consented. (This was the cause of the quarrel described earlier, when Michelangelo had to leave Rome as he would not let the Pope see what he was painting.) Now when a third of the work was completed (as I found out from Michelangelo himself, to clear up any uncertainty) during the winter when the north wind was blowing several spots of mould started to appear on the surface. The reason for this was that the Roman lime, which is white in colour and made of travertine, does not dry very quickly, and when mixed with pozzolana,* which is a brownish colour, forms a dark mixture which is very watery before it sets; then after the wall has been thoroughly soaked, it often effloresces when it is drying. Thus this salt efflorescence appeared in many places, although in time the air dried it up. When Michelangelo saw what was happening he despaired of the whole undertaking and was reluctant to go on. However, his holiness sent Giuliano da Sangallo to see him and explain the reason for the blemishes. Sangallo explained how to remove the moulds and encouraged him to continue. Then, when the work was half finished, the Pope who had subsequently gone to inspect it several times (being helped up the ladders by Michelangelo) wanted it to be thrown open to the public. Being hasty and impatient by nature, he simply could not bear to wait until it was perfect and had, so to say, received the final touch.

As soon as it was thrown open, the whole of Rome flocked to see it; and the Pope was the first, not having the patience to wait till the dust had settled after the dismantling of the scaffolds. Raphael da Urbino (who had great powers of imitation) changed his style as soon as he had seen Michelangelo's work and straight away, to show his skill, painted the prophets and sibyls of Santa Maria della Pace; and Bramante subsequently tried to persuade the Pope to let Raphael paint the other half of the chapel. When Michelangelo heard about this he complained of Bramante and revealed to the Pope, without reserve, many faults in his life and in his architectural works. (He himself, as it happened, was later to correct the mistakes made by Bramante in the fabric of St Peter's.) However, the Pope recognized Michelangelo's genius more clearly every day and wanted him to carry on the work himself; and after he had seen it displayed he was of the opinion that Michelangelo would do the other half even better. And so in twenty months Michelangelo brought the project to perfect

* A volcanic dust found near Pozzuoli.

44

completion without the assistance even of someone to grind his colours. Michelangelo at times complained that because of the haste the Pope imposed on him he was unable to finish it in the way he would have liked; for his holiness was always asking him importunately when it would be ready. On one of these occasions Michelangelo retorted that the ceiling would be finished 'when it satisfies me as an artist'.

And to this the Pope replied: 'And we want you to satisfy us and finish it soon.'

Finally, the Pope threatened that if Michelangelo did not finish the ceiling quickly he would have him thrown down from the scaffolding. Then Michelangelo, who had good reason to fear the Pope's anger, lost no time in doing all that was wanted; and after taking down the rest of the scaffolding he threw the ceiling open to the public on the morning of All Saints' Day, when the Pope went into the chapel to sing Mass, to the satisfaction of the entire city.

Michelangelo wanted to retouch some parts of the painting *a secco*, as the old masters had done on the scenes below, painting backgrounds, draperies and skies in ultramarine, and in certain places adding ornamentation in gold, in order to enrich and heighten the visual impact.* The Pope, learning that this ornamentation was lacking, and hearing the work praised so enthusiastically by all who saw it, wanted him to go ahead. However, he lacked the patience to rebuild the scaffolding, and so the ceiling stayed as it was. His holiness used to see Michelangelo often and he would ask him to have the chapel enriched with colours and gold, since it looked impoverished. And Michelangelo would answer familiarly:

'Holy Father, in those days men did not bedeck themselves in gold and those you see painted there were never very rich. They were holy men who despised riches.'

For this work Michelangelo was paid by the Pope three thousand

* *Fresco secco* – as opposed to *buon fresco* – is painted on dry plaster and was rarely used, even for retouching, by Michelangelo's time.

crowns in several instalments, of which he had to spend twenty-five on colours. He executed the frescoes in great discomfort, having to work with his face looking upwards, which impaired his sight so badly that he could not read or look at drawings save with his head turned backwards; and this lasted for several months afterwards. I can talk from personal experience about this, since when I painted five rooms in the great apartments of Duke Cosimo's palace if I had not made a chair where I could rest my head and relax from time to time I would never have finished; even so this work so ruined my sight and injured my head that I still feel the effects, and I am astonished that Michelangelo bore all that discomfort so well. In fact, every day the work moved him to greater enthusiasm, and he was so spurred on by his own progress and improvements that he felt no fatigue and ignored all the discomfort.

The painting on the ceiling of the chapel is arranged with six pendentives on either side and one in the centre of the walls at the foot and the head; and on these Michelangelo painted prophets and sibyls, twelve feet high.* In the middle of the vault he depicted from the Creation up to the Flood and the Drunkenness of Noah; and in the lunettes he showed all the Ancestors of Jesus Christ. For the foreshortenings in these compartments he used no consistent rule of perspective, nor is there any fixed point of view. He accommodated the various compartments to the figures, rather than his figures to the compartments, for he was resolved to execute both the draped figures and the nudes so that they should demonstrate the perfect quality of his draughtsmanship. There is no other work to compare with this for excellence, nor could there be; and it is scarcely possible even to

* In fact, five pendentives on either side. Vasari's description, however, is substantially accurate, though in describing the histories he follows the logical sequence of the frescoes rather than the order in which they were painted. Michelangelo started work on the ceiling in 1508, the frescoes were unveiled in the summer of 1511, and the project was completed in 1512, setting the seal on his reputation as the greatest living artist.

imitate what Michelangelo accomplished. The ceiling has proved a veritable beacon to our art, of inestimable benefit to all painters, restoring light to a world that for centuries had been plunged into darkness. Indeed, painters no longer need to seek new inventions, novel attitudes, clothed figures, fresh ways of expression, different arrangements, or sublime subjects, for this work contains every perfection possible under those headings. In the nudes, Michelangelo displayed complete mastery: they are truly astonishing in their perfect foreshortenings, their wonderfully rotund contours, their grace, slenderness, and proportion. And to show the vast scope of his art he made them of all ages, some slim and some full-bodied, with varied expressions and attitudes, sitting, turning, holding festoons of oak-leaves and acorns (to represent the emblem of Pope Julius and the fact that his reign marked the golden age of Italy, before the travail and misery of the present time). The nudes down the middle of the ceiling hold medallions painted like gold or bronze with subjects taken from the Book of Kings. Moreover, to show the perfection of art and the greatness of God, in the histories Michelangelo depicted God dividing Light from Darkness, showing him in all his majesty as he rests self-sustained with arms outstretched, in a revelation of love and creative power.

In the second history, with beautiful judgement and skill he showed the Creation of the Sun and the Moon, depicting God, supported by many *putti*, in an attitude of sublime power conveyed by the strong foreshortening of his arms and legs. In the same scene Michelangelo showed the Almighty after the Blessing of the Earth and the Creation of the Animals, when he is seen on the vaulting in the form of a foreshortened figure, flying through the air, which turns and changes direction as one walks about the chapel. The same happens in the next history, where God is dividing the Waters from the Earth. And both these figures are beautiful forms and refinements of genius that only the inspired hands of Michelangelo could create. Then he went on to the Creation of Adam, where he showed God being borne by a group of nude angels of tender age who appear to be bearing up not one figure alone but the weight of the world; and this effect is achieved by the venerable majesty of the Divine Form and the way in which he moves, embracing some of the *putti* with one arm, as if to support himself, while with the other he stretches out his right hand towards Adam, a figure whose beauty, pose, and contours are such that it seems to have been fashioned that very moment by the first and supreme creator rather than by the drawing and brush of a mortal man. Beyond this in another scene he showed God taking our mother Eve from the side of Adam; and here we see the two nude figures, one so enslaved by sleep that it seems dead, and the other awakened to life by the divine benediction. The brush of this wonderfully ingenious craftsman arrestingly reveals the difference that there is between sleep and wakefulness and how the divine majesty can be portrayed in the firm and tangible terms that humans understand.

After this comes the scene when Adam, at the persuasion of a figure half woman and half serpent, brings death upon himself and upon us through the apple; and there again we see Adam and Eve, now being driven from Paradise by the angel who appears in sublime grandeur to execute the commands of a wrathful Lord. Adam displays his remorse at having sinned and his fear of death; and the woman also shows her shame, abasement, and desire for forgiveness, as she covers her breasts with her arms, pressing her hands palm to palm and sinking her neck on to her bosom, and turns her head towards the angel, showing more fear of the justice of God than hope of divine mercy. No less beautiful is the scene showing the sacrifice of Cain and Abel, where there are some figures bringing the wood, some bending down and blowing the fire, and others cutting the throat of the victim; and this Michelangelo executed as carefully and judiciously as the others. He displayed similar art and judgement in the history of the Flood, where there are depicted some dying men who are overwhelmed by terror and dismay at what has happened and in various ways are striving their utmost to find safety. For in the heads of these figures one sees life in prey to death, along with fear, dismay, and hopelessness. Michelangelo also showed the pious actions of many people who are helping one another to climb to safety to the top of a rock. Among them is a man who has clasped someone who is half dead and is striving his utmost to save him; and nothing better than this could be seen in living nature. Nor can I describe how well expressed is the story of Noah, who is shown drunk with wine and exposed, in the presence of one son who is laughing at him and two others who are covering him up: a scene of beautiful artistry that sets its own standards. Then, as if Michelangelo's genius were emboldened by what he had already done, it soared even higher and achieved even more in the five sibyls and seven prophets that are painted on the ceiling. These figures, each ten feet or more in height, are shown in varied attitudes, wearing a variety of vestments and beautiful draperies; they are all executed with marvellous judgement, and invention, and they appear truly inspired to whoever studies their attitudes and expressions.

Thus, Jeremiah can be seen with his legs crossed, holding one hand to his beard and resting an elbow on his knee; the other hand rests on his lap, and the manner in which he inclines his head clearly expresses his melancholy and anxious reflection, and the bitterness forced on him by his people. Equally fine are the two *putti* and the first sybil beyond him, in the direction of the door. In this figure Michelangelo was anxious to express the spirit of old age itself; she is enveloped in draperies, to suggest that her blood had frozen with the passing of time. And since her sight has failed, Michelangelo has depicted her holding the book she reads very close to her eyes. Beyond this figure follows the prophet Ezekiel, an old man, full of movement and grace, and holding in one hand a roll of prophecies while he raises the other and, as he turns his head, prepares to utter words of lofty significance. Behind him there are two *putti* holding his books.

Next to him there follows a sybil who, in contrast to the Erythraean sybil described above, is holding a book at some distance and is about to turn one of the pages, sitting deep in contemplation, with one leg over the other, while she ponders what she must write; and then a little boy behind her blows on a burning brand to light her lamp.★ Many aspects of this figure are of exceptional loveliness: the expression of her face, her head-dress, and the arrangement of her draperies; and her arms, which are bared, are as beautiful as the rest. Beyond her Michelangelo painted the prophet Joel who, sunk within himself, has taken a scroll which he is reading with great attention and emotion; he looks like a living person who has applied his thoughts intently to the matter before him, and from his expression one can recognize that he is content with what he reads. Then over the door of the chapel Michelangelo placed the aged Zechariah who holds a book in which he is seeking something that he cannot find, crouching with one leg raised back and the other lower down, oblivious to the discomfort of this posture because of the intensity of his search. This is a figure marvellous in its old age, somewhat full in form and wearing beautiful draperies with a few folds. Then there is the (Delphic) sibyl, next towards the altar on the other side, who is displaying certain writings and who, with her little boys in attendance, is no less admirable than the others. And then beyond her we see the prophet Isaiah. He is lost in thought, and with his legs crossed he keeps one hand inside the pages of his book, to mark his place, while he rests the other elbow by the book and presses that hand to his cheek; he is called by one of the *putti* behind him, but stays motionless, turning only his head. Anyone who studies this figure, copied so faithfully from nature, the true mother of the art of painting, will find a beautifully composed work capable of teaching in full measure all the precepts to be followed by a good painter. Beyond him is the elderly (Cumaean) sibyl, a seated figure of great beauty, in an attitude

★ Vasari has transposed the two sybils: the first is the Persian sybil, and the second the Erythraean.

50

of extraordinary grace as she studies the pages of a book, with two beautiful *putti* at her side. Then comes the figure of a young man, representing Daniel, who is shown writing in a great book, copying things from certain other writings with eager intensity. As a support for the weight Michelangelo painted between Daniel's legs a *putto* who is supporting the book while he writes; and the brush of no other artist will ever paint a group as marvellous as this. The same holds true for the lovely figure of the Libyan sibyl who, having written a great volume drawn from many books, is about to rise to her feet in an attitude of womanly grace; and at one and the same time she makes as if to rise and to close the book, something most difficult, not to say impossible, for anyone but the master to have depicted.

What can I say of the four scenes in the corner-spandrels of the ceiling? In one of them, exerting all his boyish strength, there is David cutting off the head of Goliath, while some soldiers in the background look on in amazement. Just as astonishing are the beautiful attitudes of the figures in the scene at the corner opposite, where Michelangelo depicted the headless, writhing body of Holofernes and Judith placing the head on a shallow basket resting on the head of her serving-woman. This old woman is so tall that she has to stoop to allow her mistress to balance it properly; and using her hands to help support the burden and to cover it up, she turns her face towards the trunk of Holofernes which, though lifeless, draws up an arm and a leg and disturbs the silence inside the tent. This disturbance causes her terror and alarm, which are clearly seen in her expression. Altogether this is a picture composed with marvellous thought and care.

Even more beautiful and inspired than that and the other scenes is the story of the serpents of Moses, over the left-hand side of the altar. For here one sees the deadly havoc wrought by the rain of serpents as they bite and sting, and the brazen serpent itself that Moses placed upon a pole. Michelangelo vividly depicted the various deaths suffered by those who are doomed by the serpents' bites. The deadly poison is causing the death of countless men and women in terror and convulsion, not to mention the rigid legs and twisted arms of those who remain just as they were struck down, unable to move, and then again the beautifully executed heads shown shrieking and thrown back in despair. No less marvellously portrayed than the rest are those who keep their eyes fixed with heart-felt emotion on the serpent, the sight of which has already lessened their grief; among them is a woman who has been bitten and reduced to terror and who now in her great and obvious need is supported by another figure offering clear and welcome assistance.

There are more beautiful figures in the next scene, which shows Ahasuerus lying in bed and reading his chronicles. Thus, there are three men eating at a table, representing the council that was held to deliver the Jewish people and order the hanging of Haman. Haman himself was depicted in an extraordinary example of foreshortening, for Michelangelo painted the trunk that supports his person and the arm thrust forward so that they seem in living relief, the same effect being seen in the leg that Haman stretches out and the other parts of the body that bend inwards. Of all the beautiful and difficult figures executed by Michelangelo this is certainly the most beautiful and the most difficult. It would take too long to describe the various wonderful gestures and poses that he employed to illustrate the story of the Ancestors of Christ, showing the genealogy of all the Fathers beginning with the sons of Noah. And it is impossible to describe adequately all the many features of the figures in this section of Michelangelo's work: the draperies, the expressions of the heads, and the innumerable original and extraordinary fancies, all most brilliantly conceived. Every detail reflects Michelangelo's genius; all the figures are skilfully and beautifully foreshortened; and every single feature is manifestly inspired and beyond praise.

Then who is not filled with admiration and amazement at the awesome sight of Jonah, the last figure in the chapel? The vaulting naturally springs forward, following the curve of the masonry; but through the force of art it is apparently straightened out by the figure of Jonah, which bends in the opposite direction; and thus vanquished by the art of design, with its lights and shades, the ceiling even appears to recede.

What a happy age we live in! And how fortunate are our crafts-men, who have been given light and vision by Michelangelo and whose difficulties have been smoothed away by this marvellous and incomparable artist! The glory of his achievements has won them honour and renown; he has stripped away the bandage that kept their minds in darkness and shown them how to distinguish the truth from the falsehoods that clouded their understanding. You artists should thank heaven for what has happened and strive to imitate Michel-angelo in everything you do.

When the work was thrown open, the whole world came running to see what Michelangelo had done; and certainly it was such as to make everyone speechless with astonishment. Then the Pope, exalted by the results and encouraged to undertake even more grandiose enterprises, generously rewarded Michelangelo with rich gifts and money. Michelangelo used to say of the extraordinary favours he was shown that they proved that his holiness fully recognized his abilities; and if sometimes, arising out of their intimacy, the Pope did him some hurt, he would heal it with extraordinary gifts and favours. There was an instance of this when Michelangelo once asked the Pope's permission to go to Florence for the feast day of St John and wanted some money from him for the purpose, and the Pope said:

'Well, what about this chapel? When will it be finished?'

'When I can, Holy Father,' said Michelangelo.

Then the Pope struck Michelangelo with a staff he was holding and repeated:

'When I can! When I can! What do you mean? I will soon make you finish it.'

However, after Michelangelo had gone back to his house to

prepare for the journey to Florence, the Pope immediately sent his chamberlain, Cursio, with five hundred crowns to calm him down, as he was afraid that he would react in his usual unpredictable way; and the chamberlain made excuses for his holiness, explaining that such treatment was meant as a favour and a mark of affection. Then Michelangelo, because he understood the Pope's nature and, after all, loved him dearly, laughed it off, seeing that everything redounded to his profit and advantage and that the Pope would do anything to keep his friendship.

After the chapel had been finished, before the Pope was overtaken by death, his holiness commanded Cardinal Santiquattro and Cardinal Aginense, his nephew, that in the event of his death they should ensure that his tomb was finished, but on a smaller scale than first planned. So Michelangelo began work on the tomb once more, very eagerly, hoping to have done with it once for all without being hindered as much as before. (But for the rest of his life it was to bring him endless vexations and annoyances and drudgery, more than anything else he ever did; and for a long time it earned him the reputation of being ungrateful to the Pope who had loved and favoured him so much.) So Michelangelo returned to the tomb and worked there continuously; and he also found time to prepare designs for the façades of the chapel. But envious fortune decreed that this memorial, which had got off to such a good start, should never be finished. For at that time Pope Julius died and the work was abandoned because of the election of Pope Leo X. Being no less grandiose than Julius in mind and spirit, Leo determined to leave in his native city (from which he was the first Pope), to commemorate both himself and his inspired fellow-citizen Michelangelo, such marvels as only a great ruler, as he was, could undertake.★

Thus he gave orders for the completion of the façade of San

★ Here, as elsewhere, I have translated *divino* by 'inspired' rather than 'divine'. The adjective *divino* was widely used of Michelangelo during his lifetime, though Vasari does use it of other artists as well.

Lorenzo, the family church of the Medici; and this was why the tomb of Pope Julius remained unfinished, for Leo asked Michelangelo to give advice and plans and to be in charge of the project. Michelangelo resisted as firmly as he could, protesting that he was under an obligation to Santiquattro and Aginense to work on the tomb. But the Pope replied that he should forget about that as he had already taken care of it and arranged for them to release him, and he also promised that while he was in Florence Michelangelo would be able to work on the figures for the tomb, as he had already started to do. These suggestions greatly upset both the cardinals and Michelangelo, who went off in tears.

Then there followed endless discussions and arguments about the façade, on the grounds that a project of that kind should be made the responsibility of several artists; and in connexion with the architecture many craftsmen flocked to Rome to see the Pope, and designs were made by Baccio d'Agnolo, Antonio da Sangallo, Andrea and Jacopo Sansovino, and the gracious Raphael of Urbino, who was afterwards called to Florence for that purpose at the time of the Pope's visit. Thereupon, Michelangelo decided to make a model and not to accept anyone else as his guide or supervisor in the architecture of the façade. But because he refused any assistance in the event neither he nor anyone else carried out the work; and in despair the craftsmen went back to attend to their own affairs. Michelangelo, who was going to Carrara, had an order authorizing Jacopo Salviati to pay him a thousand crowns. However, when he arrived, finding Jacopo transacting business in his room with some other citizens, he refused to wait for an interview, left without saying a word, and made his way to Carrara. Meanwhile, having heard of Michelangelo's arrival but not finding him in Florence, Jacopo sent him the thousand crowns to Carrara. The courier demanded a receipt for the money, only to be told by Michelangelo that it was for the expenses of the Pope and no business of his, that he was not in the habit of writing out receipts or acknowledgements on behalf of other people, and that he could take the money back; and so in a panic the courier went back to Jacopo without a receipt. While Michelangelo was at Carrara and, thinking that he would finish it, was having marbles quarried for the tomb as well as for the façade, word came to him that Pope Leo had heard that in the mountains of Pietrasanta near Seravezza, in Florentine territory, at the top of the highest mountain, Monte Altissimo, there were marbles of the same beauty and quality as those of Carrara. Michelangelo already knew this, but it seems that he was reluctant to do anything about it since he was friendly with the Marquis Alberigo, lord of Carrara, and for his sake preferred to use marble quarried at Carrara rather than Seravezza; or else it was because he thought it would be a long drawn-out business and he would waste a lot of time on it, as did in fact happen. Anyhow, he was compelled to go to Seravezza, although he argued in opposition to the idea that it would be less convenient and more costly (as, especially at the beginning, proved to be the case) and, moreover, that perhaps the reports about the marble were mistaken. All the same the Pope refused to listen to a word. And then it became necessary to build a road several miles long through the mountains, breaking up rocks with hammers and pick-axes to obtain a level, and sinking piles in the marshy areas. Michelangelo thus spent several years carrying out the Pope's orders, and finally he excavated five columns of the size required, one of which is on the Piazza di San Lorenzo at Florence, while the others are on the seashore. And this was why the Marquis Alberigo, who saw his business ruined, subsequently became a bitter enemy of Michelangelo, although Michelangelo was in no way to blame for what happened.

As well as these columns Michelangelo excavated many other marbles – which are still in the quarries, where they have been abandoned for over thirty years. However, Duke Cosimo has now given orders for the completion of the road, of which there are two miles still to be built over difficult ground, for transporting these marbles. He has arranged as well for the construction of another road from a new quarry of excellent marble discovered by Michelangelo, so that many fine projects may be finished. In Seravezza, Michelangelo also discovered a hill of very hard and beautiful mixed stone near Stazzema, a village in the mountains; and Duke Cosimo has had built a paved road over four miles long to transport it to the sea.

To go back to Michelangelo's own life: from Carrara he returned to Florence where he wasted a great deal of time now on one thing and now on another. Then for the Medici Palace he made a model for the windows with supporting volutes that belong to the apartments at the corner. Giovanni da Udine decorated the room in stucco and painting, with results that are greatly admired; and Michelangelo gave the goldsmith Piloto instructions to make the shutters of perforated copper, which are certainly very impressive.

Michelangelo devoted many years of his life to quarrying marble, although it is true that while the blocks were being excavated he also made wax models and other things for the façade. But the project was delayed so long that the money the Pope assigned to it was spent on the war in Lombardy, and when Leo died the work was left unfinished, nothing having been accomplished save the laying of a foundation in front to support the façade and the transportation of a large column of marble from Carrara to the Piazza di San Lorenzo.

The death of Leo was a fearful blow to the arts and those who practised them, both in Florence and Rome; and while Adrian VI was Pope, Michelangelo stayed in Florence giving his attention to the tomb of Julius. Then Adrian died and was succeeded by Clement VII, who was no less anxious than Leo and his other predecessors to leave a name glorified by the arts of architecture, sculpture, and painting. It was at that time, in 1525, that Giorgio Vasari was taken as a young boy to Florence by the cardinal of Cortona and placed with Michelangelo as an apprentice. However, Michelangelo was called to Rome by Pope Clement, who was ready to have a start made on the library of San Lorenzo and the new sacristy, in which he intended to place the marble tombs he was having built for his ancestors. Before leaving, Michelangelo decided that Vasari should go to work with del Sarto until he was free again himself, and in person he Andrea took Vasari along to Andrea's workshop to introduce him.

He then left for Rome in a hurry, harassed once again by Francesco Maria, duke of Urbino, the nephew of Pope Julius, who complained that Michelangelo had received sixteen thousand crowns for the tomb and yet stayed in Florence amusing himself, and who threatened him angrily that if he did not attend to the work he would make him regret it. After Michelangelo had arrived in Rome, Pope Clement, who wanted to make use of his services, advised him to settle his account with the duke's agents, for the Pope believed that in view of all he had done Michelangelo was a creditor rather than a debtor; and that was how matters were left. After the Pope and Michelangelo had discussed many things together, they resolved to finish completely the sacristy and the new library of San Lorenzo at Florence.

So Michelangelo again left Rome and raised the cupola of the sacristy as we see it today. He designed it in a composite style and asked the goldsmith Piloto to make for it a very beautiful ball with seventy-two facets. It happened that while the cupola was being raised Michelangelo was asked by some of his friends:

'Shouldn't you make your lantern very different from that of Filippo Brunelleschi?'

'Certainly I can make it different,' he replied, 'but not better.'*

Michelangelo made in the sacristy four tombs to hold the bodies of the fathers of the two Popes: namely, the elder Lorenzo and his

---

* The old sacristy of San Lorenzo was rebuilt by Brunelleschi after the basilica had been destroyed by fire in 1423. Michelangelo became involved in plans to complete the Medici church of San Lorenzo after 1515. The first project – the creation of a façade – was abandoned; in 1520 he began planning the Medici Chapel attached to San Lorenzo; and subsequently he was commissioned to design the Laurenziana Library in the cloister. The marvellous sculptural decoration of the chapel is discussed (along with the rest of Michelangelo's work as a sculptor) by John Pope Hennessy in his *Italian High Renaissance and Baroque Sculpture* (Phaidon, 3 vols, 1963).

brother Giuliano, and those of Giuliano, the brother of Leo, and of Duke Lorenzo, Leo's nephew. He wanted to execute the work in imitation of the old sacristy made by Filippo Brunelleschi but with different decorative features; and so he did the ornamentation in a composite order, in a style more varied and more original than any other master, ancient or modern, has ever been able to achieve. For the beautiful cornices, capitals, bases, doors, tabernacles, and tombs were extremely novel, and in them he departed a great deal from the kind of architecture regulated by proportion, order, and rule which other artists did according to common usage and following Vitruvius and the works of antiquity but from which Michelangelo wanted to break away.*

The licence he allowed himself has served as a great encouragement to others to follow his example; and subsequently we have seen the creation of new kinds of fantastic ornamentation containing more of the grotesque than of rule or reason. Thus all artists are under a great and permanent obligation to Michelangelo, seeing that he broke the bonds and chains that had previously confined them to the creation of traditional forms.

Later Michelangelo sought to make known and to demonstrate his new ideas to even better effect in the library of San Lorenzo: namely, in the beautiful distribution of the windows, the pattern of the ceiling, and the marvellous entrance of the vestibule. Nor was there ever seen such resolute grace, both in detail and overall effect, as in the consoles, tabernacles, and cornices, nor any stairway more commodious. And in this stairway, he made such strange breaks in the design of the steps, and he departed in so many details and so widely from normal practice, that everyone was astonished.

It was at that time that Michelangelo sent his assistant, Pietro Urbino of Pistoia, to Rome to carry to completion a very fine figure

* Vitruvius was a Roman architect of the time of Augustus (Marcus Vitruvius Pollio) whose *De architectura libri X* – rediscovered in the fifteenth century – exercised a profound influence on Renaissance architectural theory.

of the naked Christ bearing the cross, which was placed on behalf of Antonio Metelli beside the principal chapel of Santa Maria sopra Minerva. Soon afterwards there took place the sack of Rome and the expulsion of the Medici from Florence; and with the change of government it was decided to rebuild the city's fortifications and to appoint Michelangelo as Commissary General in charge of the work. Thereupon he drew up plans and had fortifications built for several parts of the city; and finally, he encircled the hill of San Miniato with bastions. These he made not with the usual sods of earth, wood, and bundles of brushwood but with a strong, interwoven base of chestnut, oak, and other strong materials and (in place of the sods) unbaked bricks of tow and dung which were squared very carefully. Subsequently the Signoria of Florence sent him to Ferrara to inspect the fortifications of Duke Alfonso I and his artillery and munitions. The duke treated him very courteously and begged him, at his leisure, to make something for him with his own hand, and Michelangelo readily agreed to do so. Then, returning to Florence, he worked continuously on the fortification. Yet despite this distraction he secretly spent time working for the duke on a picture of Leda, which he painted with his own hand in tempera (an inspired work, as I shall describe later) and on the statues for the tombs of San Lorenzo. At this time Michelangelo also spent six months or so at San Miniato in order to hurry on the fortification of the hill, because if the enemy captured this point, the city was lost. All these enterprises he pursued with the utmost diligence. Meanwhile, he continued the work in the sacristy of San Lorenzo, in which there were seven statues which were left partly finished and partly not. Taking these and the architectural inventions of the tombs into account, it must be confessed that he surpassed all others in practice of the three arts. To be sure, the marble statues to be seen in San Lorenzo, which he blocked out or finished, provide convincing evidence for this claim. Among them is the figure of Our Lady, seated with her right leg crossed over the left and one knee placed on the other, while the child, with his thighs astride the leg that is uppermost, turns in a most enchanting attitude, looking for his mother's milk; and Our Lady, holding him with one hand and supporting herself with the other, leans forward to give it to him. Although this statue remained unfinished, having been roughed out and left showing the marks of the chisel, in the imperfect block one can recognize the perfections of the completed work. Michelangelo's ideas for the tombs of Duke Giuliano and Duke Lorenzo de' Medici caused even more astonished admiration. For here he decided that Earth alone did not suffice to give them an honourable burial worthy of their greatness but that they should be accompanied by all the parts of the world; and he resolved that their sepulchres should have around and above them four statues. So to one tomb he gave Night and Day, and to the other Dawn and Evening; and these statues are so beautifully formed, their attitudes so lovely, and their muscles treated so skilfully, that if the art of sculpture were lost they would serve to restore to it its original lustre.

Then among the other statues there are the two captains in armour: one, the pensive Duke Lorenzo, the embodiment of wisdom, with legs so finely wrought that nothing could be better; the other, Duke Giuliano, a proud figure, with the head, the throat, the setting of the eyes, the profile of the nose, the opening of the mouth, and the hair made with such inspired craftsmanship, as are the hands, the arms, the knees, the feet, and indeed every detail, that one's eyes can never be tired of gazing at it. One has only to study the beauty of the buskins and the cuirass to believe that the statue was made by other than human hands. But what shall I say of the Dawn, a nude woman who is such as to arouse melancholy in one's soul and throw sculpture into confusion? In her attitude may be seen the anxiety with which, drowsy with sleep, she rises up from her downy bed; for on awakening she has found the eyes of the great duke closed in death, and her eternal beauty is contorted with bitter sorrow as she weeps in token of her desperate grief. And what can I say of the Night, a statue not only rare but unique? Who has ever seen a work of sculpture of any period, ancient or modern, to compare with this? For in her may be seen not only the stillness of one who is sleeping but also the grief and melancholy of one who has lost something great and noble. And she may well represent the Night that covers in darkness all those who for some time thought, I will not say to surpass, but even to equal Michelangelo in sculpture and design. In this statue Michelangelo expressed the very essence of sleep. And in its honour various erudite people wrote many Latin verses and rhymes in the vernacular, of which the following, by an unknown author, is an example:

The Night that you see sleeping in such loveliness was by an angel carved in this rock; and by her sleeping she has life; wake her, if you disbelieve, and she will speak to you.

To this, speaking in the person of Night, Michelangelo replied:

Dear to me is sleep, and dearer to be of stone while wrongdoing and shame prevail; not to see, not to hear, is a great blessing: so do not awaken me; speak softly.

To be sure, if the enmity that exists between fortune and genius, between the envy of the one and the skill of the other, had allowed this work to be completed, then art would have demonstrated that it surpassed nature in every way. However, in 1529, while Michelangelo was labouring with intense love and solicitude on these works, Florence was besieged, and this decisively frustrated their completion. Because of the siege Michelangelo did little or no more work on the statues, because he had been given by the Florentines the task of fortifying both the hill of San Miniato and, in addition, as I said, the city itself. After he had lent a thousand crowns to the Republic and found himself elected one of the Nine of the Militia (a council appointed for the war) Michelangelo turned all his thoughts and energies to the job of perfecting the fortifications. But in the end, when the enemy army had closed round the city, with all hope of relief gradually fading and the difficulties of resistance increased, realizing that he was in grave personal danger Michelangelo resolved to save himself by leaving Florence for Venice. So, in secret, he left quietly by way of the hill of San Miniato, taking with him his pupil Antonio Mini and his loyal friend, the goldsmith Piloto. Each of them carried a number of crowns, sewn into his quilted doublet, and having reached Ferrara they decided to stay there. It happened that because of the tumult caused by the war and the alliance between the emperor and the Pope, who were besieging Florence, Duke Alfonso d'Este was keeping close watch in Ferrara, wanting to know from those who gave lodgings to travellers the names of all arrivals from day to day; and every day he had brought to him a description of all foreign visitors and where they came from. So when Michelangelo dismounted with his companions, intending to stay in Ferrara without making himself known, his arrival was notified to the duke, who was delighted to hear the news since he already enjoyed his friendship. Alfonso (a magnanimous ruler, who all his life took great pleasure in the arts) at once sent some of the notables of his court with instructions to conduct Michelangelo in the name of his excellency to the palace, to move there his horses and all his baggage, and give him comfortable quarters. Finding himself in the power of another, Michelangelo had no other course but to submit with a good grace; and so he went with them to see the duke, although he left his belongings at the inn. The duke chided him for his aloofness, but then welcomed him very warmly and gave him a number of costly gifts; then he tried to persuade him to stay in his service in Ferrara, promising to pay him a generous salary. Michelangelo, however, who had other plans, was unwilling to remain; so the duke begged him to stay at least while the war continued and renewed the offer to give him anything in his power. Not wanting to be outdone in courtesy, Michelangelo thanked him warmly and then, turning towards his two companions, said that he had brought twelve thousand crowns to Ferrara and that if the duke needed them they were at his disposal, along with himself. After this the duke led him on a tour of the palace,

63

as he had done on a previous occasion, showing him all the fine works of art in his possession, including his own portrait by Titian which Michelangelo enthusiastically praised. However, the duke could not persuade him to stay in the palace and Michelangelo insisted on going back to the inn; whereupon the innkeeper received through the duke any number of things with which to do Michelangelo honour and was told not to accept any payment when he left.

From Ferrara Michelangelo went to Venice, where he stayed on the island of Giudecca; he left again, however, after he had been much sought after by various people in society, as he always had a low opinion of their understanding of his art. While he was there, it is said, he made for the city, at the request of Doge Gritti, a design for the bridge of the Rialto which was outstanding for its invention and ornamentation.

Meanwhile, he was strongly urged to return home and begged not to abandon his work in Florence, and he was sent a safe-conduct. Finally, overcome by longing for his native land, he made up his mind to go back, at some risk to himself. It was then that he finished the Leda he was painting for Duke Alfonso; and it was subsequently taken to France by his assistant, Antonio Mini. At this time Michelangelo saved the campanile of San Miniato, a tower whose two pieces of artillery had inflicted such terrible damage on the enemy's forces that the gunners in the enemy camp bombarded it with their heavy cannon. The tower was already half destroyed and would soon be a complete shambles. However, Michelangelo protected it so well with bales of wool and stout mattresses suspended by ropes that it is still standing.

They also say that during the siege of Florence Michelangelo was given the opportunity of satisfying an earlier ambition of his and obtaining a marble block from Carrara, eighteen feet high, that Pope Clement had given to Baccio Bandinelli who had also wanted it. As it was now public property Michelangelo asked the Gonfalonier for the marble, which he was given with instructions to put it to good use. Baccio had himself made a model and cut away a good part of the stone; and then when he was allocated the marble Michelangelo made a model of his own. However, after the Medici were restored to power the block was given back to Baccio. And after the treaty had been signed, Baccio Valori, the Pope's emissary, received orders to arrest and imprison some of the citizens who had been politically active; and the tribunal also sent for Michelangelo. Suspecting that this would happen, he had secretly fled to the house of one of his friends where he stayed hidden for several days until the tumult had died down. Then Pope Clement, mindful of Michelangelo's talent and ability, ordered that everything possible should be done to find him and that far from being charged he should be given back his former appointments and told to attend to the work at San Lorenzo, in charge of which Pope Clement placed as commissary Giovan-battista Figiovanni, prior of San Lorenzo, who was an old servant of the Medici family. Reassured by this, to win Baccio Valori's good-will Michelangelo then started work on a marble figure, six feet high, showing Apollo drawing an arrow from his quiver, and he carried it almost to completion. Today this statue is in the apartment of the prince of Florence, and it is a very precious work, even though it is not completely finished.★

At that time Michelangelo was visited by a gentleman from the court of Duke Alfonso of Ferrara, who having heard that he had made for him an outstanding work was anxious not to lose such a gem. When the man arrived in Florence he sought Michelangelo out and presented his letters of introduction. Michelangelo made him welcome and showed him the picture of Leda embracing the swan, with Castor and Pollux coming forth from the egg, which he had painted at one stroke in tempera. The duke's go-between, mindful of what he knew about Michelangelo's great reputation and being unable to perceive the excellence and artistry of the picture, said to him: 'Oh, but this is just a trifle.'

★ In fact, a David.

Michelangelo asked him what his own profession might be, knowing that no one can be a better judge than a man with experience of what he is criticizing. With a sneer, the courtier replied: 'I'm a dealer.' He said this believing that Michelangelo had failed to recognize him for what he was, and laughing at the idea of such a question as well as showing his scorn for the trading instincts of the Florentines. Michelangelo, who had understood what he was getting at perfectly well, retorted:

'Well, you've just made a poor deal for your master. Now get out of my sight.'

About that time his assistant Antonio Mini, who had to find dowries for his two sisters, asked for the Leda, which Michelangelo readily gave him, along with most of the wonderful cartoons and drawings he had made for it, and also two chests full of models, as well as a great number of finished cartoons and some pictures that were already painted. When Antonio took it into his head to go to France he carried all these away with him. He sold the Leda to the king of France through some merchants, and it is now at Fontainebleau; but the cartoons and designs came to grief, since he died shortly afterwards and some of them were stolen. Thus Florence suffered the grievous loss of many of Michelangelo's great works. Subsequently, the cartoon of the Leda was returned to Florence, and it is now in the possession of Bernardo Vecchietti; similarly, four pieces of the cartoons for the chapel, with nudes and prophets, were brought back by the sculptor Benvenuto Cellini, and these are in the hands of the heirs of Girolamo degli Albizzi.

It became necessary for Michelangelo to go to Rome to serve Pope Clement who, although angry with him, as a friend of talented men forgave him everything. The Pope gave him instructions to return to Florence and finish the library and sacristy of San Lorenzo; and to save time, a considerable number of statues that were to be included were allocated to various other sculptors. Michelangelo allocated two of them to Tribolo, one to Raffaello da Montelupo, and one to

Fra Giovanni Angelo of the Servites; and he assisted these sculptors in the work, making for them the rough clay models. They all set to with a will, and meanwhile Michelangelo had the library itself attended to. Thus the ceiling was finished with carved woodwork, executed from Michelangelo's models by the Florentines Carota and Tasso, who were excellent carpenters and masters of wood-carving; and similarly the bookshelves were designed by Michelangelo and executed by Battista del Cinque and his friend Ciappino, who were skilled in that kind of work. To enhance the work still more, there was brought to Florence the inspired artist Giovanni da Udine, who with some of his own assistants and various Florentine craftsmen decorated the tribune with stucco. So with great solicitude everyone worked hard to bring the project to completion.

Michelangelo was preparing to have the statues carried into execution; but at that very time the Pope took it into his head to have him near him in person, as he wanted to have painted the walls of the Sistine Chapel, where Michelangelo had painted the ceiling for Julius II, who was the nephew of Sixtus. On the principal wall behind the altar, Clement wanted him to paint the Last Judgement, and he was determined that it should be a masterpiece. On the opposite wall, over the main door, he had commanded that Michelangelo should depict a scene showing Lucifer driven from heaven as a punishment for his pride and hurled with all the angels who had sinned with him into the depths of hell. (It was found that many years before Michelangelo had made various drawings and sketches for these subjects, of which subsequently one was executed in the church of Santissima Trinità in Rome by a Sicilian painter who had spent many months working for him and grinding his colours. This work is in the transept of the church, in the chapel of St Gregory. It was painted in fresco, with very poor results. However, one can glimpse a certain diversity and awesomeness in the groups of nudes as they rain down from heaven to turn into demons of weird and frightening appearance on reaching the centre of the earth: certainly a strange flight of the imagination.)*

While Michelangelo was making preparations to execute the cartoons and drawings for the Last Judgement on the first wall, never a day passed without his being troubled by the agents of the duke of Urbino, who alleged that he had received sixteen thousand crowns from Pope Julius to execute his tomb. This accusation was more than he could bear, and, indeed, he was determined that one day he would finish the tomb, even though he was already an old man. He was more than willing to stay in Rome for this purpose (now that without seeking it he had been given a pretext for not going back to Florence) because he went in great fear of Duke Alessandro de' Medici. Michelangelo was convinced that Alessandro was no friend of his; for one day when the duke had given him to understand through Alessandro Vitelli that he should select the best site for the castle and citadel of Florence, he had replied that he would only go there if he were ordered to do so by Pope Clement.

Eventually agreement was reached that the tomb should be finished in the following manner: the plan for a free-standing rect-angular tomb was scrapped, and instead only one of the original façades was to be executed, in whatever way best suited Michelangelo, and he was to include six statues from his own hand. In this contract with the duke of Urbino, his excellency consented that Michelangelo should be at the disposal of Pope Clement for four months in the year, either at Florence or wherever the Pope wanted to employ him. However, although Michelangelo thought that he would get some peace at last, he was not to finish with the tomb so easily; for Pope Clement, anxious to see the final proof of his genius, made him devote his time to the cartoon for the Last Judgement. However,

* Here and elsewhere I have usually translated *terribile* by 'awesome' or 'sublime'. The *terribilità* of Michelangelo's style and subjects was recognized by many of his contemporaries. The implications of the word are discussed by Robert J. Clements in *Michelangelo's Theory of Art* (Routledge and Kegan Paul, 1963).

although he convinced the Pope that he was working on that, he also kept working in secret, as hard as he could, on the statues for the tomb.

Then in 1534 came the death of Pope Clement, and thereupon work ceased on the sacristy and library at Florence which had remained unfinished despite the effort that had gone into them. Michelangelo was now fully convinced that he would be free to give all his time to finishing the tomb of Julius II. But after Paul III had been elected, before no time at all he had Michelangelo summoned before him and after paying him compliments and making him various offers tried to persuade him to enter his service and remain near him. Michelangelo refused, saying that he was bound under contract to the duke of Urbino until the tomb of Julius was finished. Then the Pope grew angry and said:

'I have nursed this ambition for thirty years, and now that I'm Pope am I not to have it satisfied? I shall tear the contract up. I'm determined to have you in my service, no matter what.'

When he saw the Pope's determination, Michelangelo was tempted to leave Rome and somehow or other find a way to finish the tomb. All the same, being a prudent man and fearing the power of the Pope, he resolved to say things to please him and spin matters out (seeing the Pope was an old man) until circumstances changed. Meanwhile, the Pope was anxious to have some notable work from Michelangelo's hands, and one day, accompanied by ten cardinals, he sought him out at his home. When he arrived his holiness asked to see all the statues intended for the tomb of Julius, and he thought they were all marvellous, especially the Moses which, according to the cardinal of Mantua, was by itself enough to do honour to Pope Julius. Having seen the drawings and cartoons that Michelangelo was preparing for the chapel walls, which he thought stupendous, the Pope again begged him with great insistence to enter his service, promising that he would persuade the duke of Urbino to content himself with three statues and to have the others made from Michelangelo's models by competent artists. This was then arranged by means of his holiness with the duke's agents, a fresh contract being drawn up and confirmed by the duke. Michelangelo freely committed himself to paying for the other three statues and having the tomb erected, and for this purpose he deposited 1,580 ducats with the Strozzi bank. He need not have taken this step; and certainly he now considered that he had done enough to free himself of that tedious and worrisome project. And then he had the tomb erected in San Pietro in Vincoli, as follows:

At the foot, he placed an ornamental base with four projections accommodating four terminal figures in place of the four Captives which were planned originally. Since this substitution impoverished the lower storey, he placed at the foot of each of the figures a reversed console resting on a pedestal. Between the four terminals there were three niches, two of which (at the sides) were circular and were to have contained the Victories. Instead of the Victories, however, in one of the niches he placed a figure of Leah, the daughter of Laban, to represent the Active Life: in one hand she held a looking-glass, to signify the deliberation with which we should conduct our affairs, and in the other a garland of flowers, signifying the talents that adorn our life on earth and glorify it after death. In the other niche he placed a figure of Leah's sister, Rachel, representing the Contemplative Life: with her hands clasped and one knee slightly bent, she wears an expression of rapture on her face. Michelangelo executed these statues himself, in less than a year. In the centre, in the original plan, there was to have been one of the doors leading into the little oval temple containing the quadrangular sarcophagus; instead, there was a rectangular niche, containing a marble dado which supported the gigantic and wonderfully beautiful statue of Moses, of which enough has already been said. Over the heads of the terminal figures, which act as capitals, are the architrave, the frieze, and the cornice, projecting over the terminals and richly carved with foliage, ovolo mouldings, and dentils, and matched by other rich ornamentation. Then above the cornice is the upper storey of the façade, with four other kinds of terminal figures placed perpendicularly over those of the lower storey and taking the form of unadorned pilasters surmounted by differently moulded cornices. This part of the façade corresponds in its various details with the lower storey, and thus Michelangelo made an opening (to match the niche containing the statue of Moses) in which, resting on the projections of the lower cornice, was placed a marble sarcophagus bearing the recumbent statue of Pope Julius II, which was executed by the sculptor Tommaso Boscoli. In the niche beyond the figure of Julius is a statue of Our Lady holding the child in her arms, executed from Michelangelo's model by the sculptor Scherano da Settignano. Both these figures are tolerably good. In the other two rectangular niches (over the statues of the Contemplative Life and the Active Life) are respectively a sybil and a prophet, both seated, which were made by Raffaello da Montelupo, as is described in the *Life* of his father, Baccio; but these were little to Michelangelo's liking. At the summit, the façade was given another kind of cornice projecting like the cornice of the lower storey over the front of the work. Resting on this, over the terminal figures, were marble candelabra; and in the middle, above the prophet and the sybil, was the coat-of-arms of Pope Julius. Then in the spaces of the niches windows were built for the convenience of the friars who served the church so that, as the choir was placed behind the tomb, their voices could be heard and they could see divine service being celebrated. Altogether the tomb succeeded very well, although it was not as impressive as planned originally.

Since he could hardly do otherwise, Michelangelo resolved to enter the service of Pope Paul, who wanted him to continue with the work commissioned by Pope Clement without changing anything in the inventions and general conception of what had been decided, such was the Pope's respect for his great talents. Indeed, Pope Paul felt for Michelangelo such reverence and love that he always went out of his way to please him. For example, his holiness wanted to have his own coat-of-arms painted under the Jonah in the chapel, in place of the arms of Pope Julius; but when this suggestion was put to Michelangelo, not wanting to make changes that would do wrong to Pope Julius and Pope Clement, he would not agree, saying that his coat-of-arms would not look well there. And his holiness, to avoid offending him, accepted his decision. To be sure, the Pope fully appreciated Michelangelo's excellence and realized that he always did what was just and honourable, without any adulation or respect of persons: something which rulers rarely come across.

For the wall of the chapel, overhanging about a foot from the summit, Michelangelo then had carefully built a projection of bricks, which had been especially chosen and baked, to prevent any dust or dirt from settling on the painting. I shall not dwell on the details of the inventions and composition of the Last Judgement, since so many copies of all sizes have been printed that there is no call to waste time describing it. It is enough for us to understand that this extraordinary man chose always to refuse to paint anything save the human body in its most beautifully proportioned and perfect forms and in the greatest variety of attitudes, and thereby to express the wide range of the soul's emotions and joys. He was content to prove himself in the field in which he was superior to all his fellow craftsmen, painting his nudes in the grand manner and displaying his great understanding of the problems of design. Thus he has demonstrated how painting can achieve facility in its chief province: namely, the reproduction of the human form. And concentrating on this subject he left to one side the charm of colouring and the caprices and novel fantasies of certain minute and delicate refinements that many other artists, and not without reason, have not entirely neglected. For some artists, lacking Michelangelo's profound knowledge of design, have tried by using a variety of tints and shades of colour, by including in their work various novel and bizarre inventions (in brief, by following the other method of painting) to win themselves a place among the most distinguished masters. But Michelangelo, standing always firmly rooted in his profound understanding of the art, had shown those who can understand how they should achieve perfection.

To return to the Last Judgement: Michelangelo had already finished more than three-fourths of the work when Pope Paul went to see it. On this occasion Biagio da Cesena, the master of ceremonies and a very scrupulous person, happened to be with the Pope in the chapel and was asked what he thought of the painting. He answered that it was most disgraceful that in so sacred a place there should have been depicted all those nude figures, exposing themselves so shamefully, and that it was no work for a papal chapel but rather for the public baths and taverns. Angered by this comment, Michelangelo determined he would have his revenge; and as soon as Biagio had left he drew his portrait from memory in the figure of Minos, shown with a great serpent curled round his legs, among a heap of devils in hell; nor for all his pleading with the Pope and Michelangelo could Biagio have the figure removed, and it was left, to record the incident, as it is today.

It then happened that Michelangelo fell no small distance from the scaffolding in the chapel and hurt his leg; and in his pain and anger he refused to be treated by anyone. Now at this time there lived a certain Florentine called Baccio Rontini, a friend and admirer of Michelangelo's and an ingenious physician. Feeling sorry for Michelangelo, one day he went along to see him at home; when he received no answer to his knocking, either from Michelangelo or the neighbours, he made his way up by a secret way from room to room until he found Buonarroti, who was in a desperate condition. And then Baccio refused to go away or leave his side until he was better. After he was cured, Michelangelo returned to the chapel and worked continuously until everything was finished. And the paintings he did were imbued with such force that he justified the words of Dante: 'Dead are the dead, the living truly live. . . .'* We are shown the misery of the damned and the joy of the blessed.

* *Morti li morti, e i vivi paren vivi. Purgatory* xii, 67.

When the Last Judgement was revealed it was seen that Michelangelo had not only excelled the masters who had worked there previously but had also striven to excel even the vaulting that he had made so famous; for the Last Judgement was finer by far, and in it Michelangelo outstripped himself. He imagined to himself all the terror of those days and he represented, for the greater punishment of those who have not lived well, the entire Passion of Jesus Christ, depicting in the air various naked figures carrying the cross, the column, the lance, the sponge, the nails, and the crown of thorns. These were shown in diverse attitudes and were perfectly executed with consummate facility. We see the seated figure of Christ turning towards the damned his stern and terrible countenance in order to curse them; and in great fear Our Lady draws her mantle around her as she hears and sees such tremendous desolation. In a circle around the figure of Christ are innumerable prophets and apostles; and most remarkable are the figures of Adam and St Peter, included, it is believed, as being respectively the original parent of the human race that is now brought to Judgement and the first foundation of the Christian Church. At the feet of Christ is a most beautiful St Bartholomew, who is displaying his flayed skin. We see also the nude figure of St Lawrence, and in addition an endless number of male and female saints and other figures of men and women around Christ, near or distant, who embrace each other and rejoice, because they have won everlasting beatitude by the grace of God and as a reward for their good deeds. Beneath the feet of Christ are the Seven Angels with the Seven Trumpets as described by St John the Evangelist; as they sound the call to Judgement they cause the hair of those who are looking at them to stand on end at the terrible wrath of their countenances. Among the rest are two angels with the Book of Life in their hands; and near them on one side, depicted with perfect judgement, may be seen the seven mortal sins in the form of devils, assailing and striving to drag down to hell the souls that are flying towards heaven, all striking the most beautiful attitudes and wonderfully foreshortened.

Nor did Michelangelo hesitate to show to the world, in the resurrection of the dead, how they take to themselves once more bones and flesh from the same earth and how with the help of others already alive, they go soaring towards heaven, where again they are assisted by the souls of those already blessed; and all this was painted with the appropriate judgement and consideration. Throughout the painting may be seen exercises and studies of various kinds, the perfection of which is clearly illustrated by a notable detail showing the bark of Charon. In an attitude of frenzy, Charon is striking with his oar the souls being dragged into his bark by the demons. Here, Michelangelo was following the description given by his favourite poet, Dante, when he wrote:

> *Charon, his eyes red like a burning brand,*
> *Thumps with his oar the lingerers that delay,*
> *And rounds them up, and beckons with his hand.* ⋆

Michelangelo painted the heads of his demons with such marvellous force and variety that they are truly like monsters out of hell. And in the figures of the damned we can see the presence of sin and the fear of eternal punishment. Apart from the beauty of its every detail, it is extraordinary to see how this painting produces in its finished state an impression of such harmony that it seems to have been executed all in one day, and even so with a finish unrivalled by any miniature. To be sure, the awesomeness and grandeur of this painting, with its vast host of figures, are so overwhelming that it defies description; for in it may be seen marvellously portrayed all the emotions that mankind can experience. The discerning eye can easily distinguish the proud and the envious, the avaricious, the lustful, and other sinners of various kinds; for in this painting Michelangelo observed all the rules of decorum, and gave his figures the appropriate expressions, attitudes, and settings. This was a great and wonderful achievement; but it was all the same well within his powers, because he was always shrewd and observant and he had seen a lot of mankind,

⋆ Canto III, *Inferno* (Sayers's translation).

and thus he had acquired by contact with the day-to-day world the understanding that philosophers obtain from books and speculation. To any discerning critic the Last Judgement demonstrates the sublime force of art and Michelangelo's figures reveal thoughts and emotions that only he has known how to express. Moreover, anyone in a position to judge will also be struck by the amazing diversity of the figures which is reflected in the various and unusual gestures of the young and old, the men and the women. All these details bear witness to the sublime power of Michelangelo's art, in which skill was combined with a natural inborn grace. Michelangelo's figures stir the emotions of people who know nothing about painting, let alone those who understand. The foreshortenings that appear to be in actual relief; the way he blended his colours to produce a mellow softness and grace; and the delicate finish he gave to every detail: these serve to show the kind of picture that a good and true artist should paint. In the contours of the forms turned in a manner no other artists could have rivalled Michelangelo showed the world the true Judgement and the true Damnation and Resurrection.

The Last Judgement must be recognized as the great exemplar of the grand manner of painting, directly inspired by God and enabling mankind to see the fateful results when an artist of sublime intellect infused with divine grace and knowledge appears on earth. Behind this work, bound in chains, follow all those who believe they have mastered the art of painting; the strokes with which Michelanglo outlined his figures make every intelligent and sensitive artist wonder and tremble, no matter how strong a draughtsman he may be. When other artists study the fruits of Michelangelo's labours, they are thrown into confusion by the mere thought of what manner of things all other pictures, past or future, would look like if placed side by side with this masterpiece. How fortunate they are, and what happy memories they have stored up, who have seen this truly stupendous marvel of our times! And we can count Pope Paul III as doubly fortunate and happy, seeing that, by allowing this work to come into existence under his protection, God ensured future renown for his holiness and for Michelangelo. How greatly are the merits of the Pope enhanced by the genius of the artist! The birth of Michelangelo was indeed a stroke of fortune for all artists of the present age, for his work as a painter, a sculptor, and an architect has with its brilliance illuminated every problem and difficulty.

Michelangelo laboured for eight years on the Last Judgement, and he threw it open to view, I believe, on Christmas Day in the year 1541, to the wonder and astonishment of the whole of Rome, or rather the whole world. That year, I went to Rome myself, travelling from Venice, in order to see it; and I along with the rest was stupefied by what I saw.

As I described in the *Life* of Antonio da Sangallo, Pope Paul had caused a chapel called the Pauline to be built on the same floor, in imitation of that of Nicholas V; and for this he decided that Michelangelo should paint two large pictures containing two great scenes. In one of the pictures, therefore, Michelangelo painted the Conversion of St Paul, with Jesus Christ above and a multitude of nude angels making the most graceful movements, while below, dazed and terrified, Paul has fallen from his horse to the ground. His soldiers are about him, some trying to lift him to his feet, others dazed by the splendour and the voice of Christ shown with panic-stricken movements and striking the most beautiful and varied attitudes as they take to flight. The horse as it runs off is shown carrying along in its headlong course the man who is trying to restrain it. And all this scene is composed with extraordinary skill and draughtsmanship. The other scene contains the Crucifixion of St Peter, who is depicted in a figure of rare beauty fastened naked upon the cross, while those who are crucifying him, having made a hole in the ground, are straining to raise the cross on high, so as to crucify him with his feet in the air. Here, too, there are many remarkably judicious and beautiful details. As has been said elsewhere, Michelangelo concentrated his energies on achieving absolute perfection in what he could do best, so there are no landscapes to be seen in these scenes, nor any trees, buildings, or other embellishments and variations; for he never spent time on such things, lest perhaps he should degrade his genius. These scenes, which he painted at the age of seventy-five, were the last pictures he did; and they cost him a great deal of effort, because painting, especially in fresco, is no work for men who have passed a certain age.

Michelangelo arranged that Perin del Vaga, an accomplished painter, should decorate the vaulting with stucco and various paintings, following his own designs, and this was also the wish of Pope Paul III; but the work was afterwards delayed and nothing more was done (so many projects are left unfinished, partly because of irresolution on the part of artists and partly because of the failure of their patrons to urge them on).

Pope Paul had made a start with fortifying the Borgo and he then summoned many gentlemen, along with Antonio da Sangallo, to a conference; he wanted Michelangelo to take part as well, since he knew that it was he who had planned the fortifications around the hill of San Miniato. After considerable discussion, therefore, Michelangelo was asked to say what his opinion was, and he spoke his mind freely, although he disagreed both with Sangallo and with many of the others. Whereupon, Sangallo told him that his profession was sculpture and painting, and not fortification. Michelangelo replied that of those he knew only little, but as for fortification, given the amount of thought he had devoted to it and the practical experience he had had, he considered he knew more than Sangallo or any of his family. Then he demonstrated to him, in the presence of all the others, that he had made many errors; and as the arguments flew back and forth the Pope had to call for silence. Not long after this meeting, Michelangelo brought the Pope a plan for all the fortifications of the Borgo, which formed the basis of everything that was subsequently decided and put into effect. This was why the great gate of Santo Spirito, which was approaching completion under Sangallo's supervision, remained unfinished.

The spirit and genius of Michelangelo could not remain idle; and so, since he was unable to paint, he set to work on a piece of marble, intending to carve four figures in the round and larger than life-size (including a dead Christ) to amuse and occupy himself and also, as he used to say himself, because using the hammer kept his body healthy. This Christ, taken down from the cross, is supported by Our Lady, by Nicodemus (planted firmly on his feet as he bends down and assists her) and by one of the Marys who also gives her help on perceiving the failing strength of his mother, whose grief makes the burden intolerable. Nowhere else can one see a dead form to compare with this figure of Christ; he is shown sinking down with his limbs hanging limp and he lies in an attitude altogether different not only from that of any other of Michelangelo's figures but from that of any other figure ever made. This work, the fruit of intense labour, was a rare achievement in a single stone and truly inspired; but, as will be told later on, it remained unfinished and suffered many misfortunes, although Michelangelo had intended it to go at the foot of the altar where he hoped to place his own tomb.

It happened that in 1546 Antonio da Sangallo died; and since there was now no one supervising the building of St Peter's various suggestions were made by the superintendents to the Pope as to who should take over. At length (inspired I feel sure by God) his holiness resolved to send for Michelangelo; but when he was asked to take Sangallo's place Michelangelo refused, saying, to excuse himself, that architecture was not his vocation. In the end, entreaties being of no avail, the Pope commanded him to accept. So to his intense dismay and completely against his will Michelangelo was compelled to embark on this enterprise. Then one day or other he made his way to St Peter's to have a look at the model in wood that Sangallo had made and to study the building itself. When he arrived he found there all the Sangallo faction who, crowding before him, said as agreeably as they could that they were delighted that he had been given responsibility for the building, and that Sangallo's model was certainly like a meadow where there would never be any lack of pasture.

'That's only too true,' observed Michelangelo; and by this (as he told a friend) he meant to imply that it provided pasture for dumb oxen and silly sheep who knew nothing about art. And afterwards he used to say openly that Sangallo's model was deficient in lights, that on the exterior Sangallo had made too many rows of columns one above another, and that with all its projections, spires, and subdivisions of members it derived more from the German manner than from either the sound method of the ancient world or the graceful and lovely style followed by modern artists. As well as this, he would add, fifty years of time and over three hundred thousand crowns of money could be saved on the building, which could also be executed with more majesty, grandeur, and facility, better ordered design, and greater beauty and convenience. Subsequently, Michelangelo convincingly demonstrated the truth of his words with a model he made himself, and which showed the building completed on the lines we can see today. This model cost him twenty-five crowns and it was made in a fortnight. In contrast, Sangallo's (as I said earlier) cost four thousand and took many years. And from these and various other circumstances it became evident that the building had been turned into a shop organized for making money on behalf of those who were trying to monopolize the work, which they were dragging out indefinitely. These methods were more than repugnant to a man of Michelangelo's rectitude; and, in order to get rid of the culprits, when the Pope was pressing him to accept the position of chief architect he said to them openly one day that they should enlist the help of their friends and do everything in their power to prevent his being put in charge. For if he were, he went on, he would refuse to allow any of them to enter the building. These words, spoken in public, were taken very badly, as may well be imagined; and they explain why they conceived for Michelangelo a bitter hatred which grew daily more intense (as they saw him change all the plans, inside and out) till they could scarcely bear to let him live. Every day, as will be described, they thought up various new ways to torment him.

Finally, the Pope issued a *motu proprio* putting Michelangelo in charge of the building, with full authority, and giving him power to do or undo whatever he chose, and to add, remove, or vary anything just as he wished; the Pope also commanded that all the officials employed there should take their orders from him.* Then Michelangelo, seeing the great trust and confidence that the Pope reposed in him, wanted to demonstrate his own good will by having it declared in the papal decree that he was devoting his time to the fabric for the love of God, and without any other reward. (It is true that the Pope had previously granted him the toll for the river-crossing at Piacenza, which yielded about six hundred crowns; but he lost it when Pier Luigi died and was given instead a chancellery at Rimini, which was worth less and meant little to him. And though the Pope several times sent him money by way of a salary he would never take it; and the truth of this is witnessed by Alessandro Ruffini, who was then chamberlain to the Pope, and Pier Giovanni Aliotto, bishop of Forlì.)

The Pope eventually gave his approval to the model Michelangelo had made. This diminished the size of St Peter's but increased its grandeur in a manner which pleases all those able to judge, although there are some who claim to be experts (without justification) and who do not approve. Michelangelo found that four principal piers, made by Bramante and retained by Antonio da Sangallo, which were to help support the weight of the cupola, were weak; so he partly filled them in, making on each side two spiral stairways up which the beasts of burden can climb with the materials, as can men on horseback, to the uppermost level of the arches. He made the first cornice above the travertine arches; this curves round gracefully and is a marvellous and distinctive piece of work, better than anything else of its kind. He also began the two great hemicycles of the crossing,

* Michelangelo's appointment as Chief Architect to St Peter's was confirmed in January 1547. He remained responsible for this tremendous undertaking until his death.

and whereas previously, under the direction of Bramante, Baldassare Peruzzi, and Raphael, as was said, eight tabernacles were being built on the side of the church facing the Campo Santo (and the same plan was followed by Sangallo) Michelangelo reduced the number to three, with three chapels behind them. Above these he placed a travertine vault and a range of windows alive with light, of varied form and sublime grandeur. However, as these things are in existence and can also be studied in engravings (Sangallo's as well as those of Michelangelo) there is no need to describe them. It is enough to record that Michelangelo as diligently as he could had the work pressed forward in those parts of the building where the design was to be changed, so that it would be impossible for anyone else to make further alterations. This was a shrewd and prudent precaution, for it is pointless doing good work without providing for what may happen later: the rash presumption of those who might be supposed to know something (if words were to be trusted more than deeds) can easily, with the approval of the ignorant, have disastrous results.

The people of Rome, with the consent of Pope Paul, were anxious to give some useful, commodious, and beautiful form to the Capitol, and in order to embellish the district, to furnish it with colonnades, with ascents, with inclined approaches with and without steps, and also with the ancient and beautiful statues that were already there. For this purpose they sought advice from Michelangelo, who made for them a very rich and beautiful design in which on the side of the Senators' Palace (on the east) he arranged a façade of travertine and a flight of steps ascending from the two sides to meet on a level space giving access to the centre of the palace hall, with ornate curving wings adorned with balusters serving as supports and parapets. Then to improve the effect he mounted on pedestals in front of the steps the two ancient figures of recumbent river gods, one representing the Tiber and the other the Nile. (Between these two rare statues, each eighteen feet long, it is intended to have a niche containing a statue of Jupiter.) On the southern side, to bring the Conservators' Palace into line he designed for it a richly adorned façade, with a portico at the foot filled with columns and niches for many ancient statues; and all around are various adornments of doors and windows, some of which are already in place. Then on the opposite side, towards the north, below the Araceli, there is to be another similar façade; and in front of this, on the west, is to be an almost level ascent of shallow steps with a balustrade. And here will be the principal entrance to the piazza with a colonnade and various bases on which will be placed the collection of ancient statues with which the Capitol is now so richly furnished. In the middle of the piazza, on an oval base, has been erected the famous bronze horse bearing the figure of Marcus Aurelius, which Pope Paul had removed from the Piazza di Laterano, where it had been put by Sixtus IV. Today work on this whole enterprise is yielding such beautiful results that it is worthy of being numbered among Michelangelo's finest achievements; and under the supervision of Tommaso de' Cavalieri (a Roman gentleman, one of the greatest friends Michelangelo ever had) it is now being brought to completion.

Pope Paul III had told Sangallo, while he was alive, to carry forward the palace of the Farnese family, but the great upper cornice, completing the outer edge of the roof, had still to be constructed, and his holiness wanted Michelangelo to undertake this and to use his own designs. Unable to refuse the Pope, who so greatly esteemed and favoured him, Michelangelo made a full-scale wood model, twelve feet long, and he caused this to be placed on one of the corners of the palace to show the effect of the finished work. His holiness and everyone else in Rome being pleased by the result, the part which can be seen now was carried to completion, producing the most beautiful and varied cornice that has ever been known in ancient or modern times. Consequently, after Sangallo died, the Pope wanted Michelangelo to take charge of the whole building as well; and so Michelangelo made the great marble window with the beautiful columns of variegated stone which is above the principal door of the palace, surmounted by a large marble coat-of-arms, of great beauty and originality, belonging to Pope Paul III, the founder of the palace. Within the palace over the first storey of the courtyard Michelangelo continued the two other storeys, with their incomparably beautiful, graceful, and varied windows, ornamentation and crowning cornice. Hence, through the labours and genius of that man, the courtyard has been transformed into the most beautiful in all Europe. He widened and enlarged the great hall and reconstructed the front corridor, making the vaulting with a new and ingenious kind of arch in the form of a half oval. Then that same year at the Baths of Antoninus was discovered a block of marble, measuring fourteen feet in every direction, in which there had been carved by the ancients a figure of Hercules standing on a mound and holding the bull by its horns, with another figure helping him, and with a surrounding group of shepherds, nymphs, and animals: a work of truly exceptional beauty, which was believed to have been meant for a fountain. Michelangelo advised that it should be taken to the second courtyard of the Farnese Palace and there restored to spout water as it did originally. This was agreed, and the work is still being carried on today with great diligence, by order of the Farnese family. At the same time Michelangelo made designs for a bridge crossing the Tiber in a straight line with the palace, so that it would be possible to go direct to another palace and gardens that they owned in the Trastevere, and also from the principal door facing the Campo di Fiore to be able to see at a glance the courtyard, the fountain, the Strada Julia, the bridge, and the beauties of the other garden, all in a straight line as far as the other door opening on to the Strada di Trastevere. This was a marvellous undertaking which was worthy of that pontiff and of Michelangelo's talent, judgement, and powers of design.

Fra Sebastiano, Keeper of the Papal Seal, died in 1547; and at that time Pope Paul proposed that the ancient statues of his palace should be restored. Michelangelo was happy to favour the Milanese sculptor Guglielmo della Porta, whom Sebastiano had recommended to him as a young man of promise; and liking his work he presented him to

Pope Paul for the restoration of the statues. Things went so well that Michelangelo obtained for him the office of Keeper of the Seal, and then a start was made on the statues, some of which can be seen in the palace today. However, forgetting the benefits he had received from Michelangelo, Guglielmo later became one of his enemies.

In 1549 there took place the death of Paul III, whereupon after the election of Pope Julius III Cardinal Farnese commissioned a great tomb to be made for Pope Paul (his kinsman) by Fra Guglielmo, who arranged to erect it in St Peter's, under the first arch of the new church beneath the tribune. This meant, however, that it would obstruct the floor of the church, and the position chosen was in fact quite wrong. So Michelangelo gave the sensible advice that it could not and should not stand there. Fra Guglielmo, thinking this was done out of envy, became filled with hatred against him. Later on, however, he came to realize that Michelangelo had spoken the truth and that he himself had been at fault because he had been given the opportunity to carry the work through and had not done so. I can testify to this myself, for in 1550 I had been ordered by Pope Julius III to go to Rome to serve him (and I went very willingly, because of my love for Michelangelo), and I took part in the discussion. Michelangelo wanted the tomb to be erected in one of the niches where the Column of the Possessed is today, which was the proper place; and I had so worked to arrange matters that Pope Julius was resolving to have his own tomb made in the other niche, with the same design as Pope Paul's, in order to balance it. But Fra Guglielmo, who opposed this scheme, brought it about that the Pope's own tomb was in the end never finished nor was that of the other pontiff; and all this was predicted by Michelangelo.

That same year Pope Julius made up his mind to have a marble chapel constructed in the church of San Pietro in Montorio with tombs for his uncle Cardinal Antonio de' Monte and for his grandfather, Fabriano, who was the founder of the greatness of his illustrious family. The designs and models for these were made by Vasari;

and then Pope Julius, who always admired Michelangelo's genius and who loved Vasari, wanted Michelangelo to settle what the price should be. For his part, Vasari begged the Pope to persuade Michelangelo to take the work under his general supervision. Now Vasari had proposed that Simone Mosca should do the carvings for this work and Raffaello da Montelupo the statues. However, Michelangelo advised against having any carved foliage, even on the architectural parts, saying that where there were marble figures nothing else was needed. Because of this Vasari feared that the finished work would be impoverished; but subsequently, when he did see it completed, he had to admit that Michelangelo had shown no little judgement. Then Michelangelo refused to let Montelupo make the statues, because he had seen how badly he had acquitted himself in those he himself had designed for the tomb of Pope Julius II. He was far happier that they should be allocated to Bartolommeo Ammanati (whom Vasari had recommended) even though he himself was at odds both with Ammanati and with Nanni di Baccio Bigio. This, as a matter of fact, had been caused by a trivial incident: for when they were boys, prompted by their love of sculpture rather than by any wish to offend him, they had gone into Michelangelo's house and stealthily filched from his servant Antonio Mini many of Michelangelo's drawings; subsequently, through the intervention of the magistrates, these were returned, and Michelangelo himself with the help of Giovanni Norchiati, canon of San Lorenzo, had saved them from any further punishment.

Discussing this escapade with Michelangelo, Vasari told him laughingly that he did not think they deserved any blame, and that if he had had the chance himself he would not merely have taken a few drawings but would have stolen everything of his that he could lay hands on in order to learn the art. One should encourage and reward those who try to improve themselves, Vasari added, and not treat them as if they had stolen someone's money or other important belongings. In this way the whole affair was turned into a joke.

So a start was made on the work for San Pietro in Montorio, and that same year Vasari and Ammanati went to bring the marbles from Carrara to Rome. Now at that time Vasari used to visit Michelangelo every day; and one morning (it being Holy Year) the Pope graciously gave them a dispensation to visit the seven churches on horseback and gain the indulgence together. While they were going from one church to another they discussed the arts very eagerly and fruitfully, and from their stimulating conversation Vasari composed a dialogue which will be published (with other material on art) at a favourable opportunity.*

That year also Pope Julius confirmed the decree issued by Pope Paul III regarding the building of St Peter's; and although members of the Sangallo clique spoke evil of Michelangelo they found the Pope unwilling to listen to a word of it. For Vasari had convinced his holiness that in fact Michelangelo had succeeded in breathing life into the building and he persuaded him to plan nothing without asking Michelangelo's advice. The Pope kept to this promise, for neither at the Villa Giulia did he do anything without finding out Michelangelo's opinion, nor in the Belvedere, when they made the existing stairway in place of the original built earlier by Bramante. (Bramante's stairway, for the principal niche in the centre of the Belvedere, consisted in two half circles with eight steps in each, a convex followed by a concave flight.) Michelangelo designed and had erected the very beautiful quadrangular staircase, with balusters of peperino-stone, which is there now.

Vasari had that year seen completed in Florence the printing of his biographies of the painters, sculptors, and architects. He had not written the biography of any living master (although there were several old artists who were still alive) with the exception of Michelangelo. And so he presented the work to Michelangelo, who received it with great pleasure. In it, in fact, were details of many things that Vasari had heard from Michelangelo's own lips, he being

* This 'dialogue' is lost.

the oldest and wisest of all the craftsmen. Then not long after, having read the work, Michelangelo sent Vasari the following sonnet which he wrote himself and which I am happy to include here in memory of his loving kindness:

> *With pen and colours you have shown how art*
> *Can equal nature. Also in a sense*
> *You have from nature snatched her eminence,*
> *Making the painted beauty touch the heart.*
>
> *Now a more worthy work your skilful hand,*
> *Writing on paper, labours and contrives –*
> *To give to those who're dead new worth, new lives;*
> *Where nature simply made, you understand.*
>
> *When men have tried in other centuries*
> *To vie with nature in the power to make,*
> *Always they had to yield to her at last.*
>
> *But you, illuminating memories,*
> *Bring back to life these lives for their own sake,*
> *And conquer nature with the vivid past.**

When Vasari left for Florence, he asked Michelangelo to prepare the work for San Pietro in Montorio. However, he also told his great friend Bindo Altoviti, who was then the consul for the Florentine colony at Rome, that it would be better to have the tombs erected in the Church of San Giovanni de' Fiorentini, that he had already suggested this to Michelangelo, who was in favour, and that this would be a good opportunity for completing the church. Bindo liked the suggestion, and being very intimate with the Pope he urged him strongly to have the chapel and tombs that his holiness was having made for Montorio put up in San Giovanni de' Fiorentini instead, adding that this would give the Florentines in Rome the

* This translation of the sonnet '*Se con lo stile e co' colori avete*' is by Elizabeth Jennings.

opportunity and incentive to meet the expense of having their church completed. If his holiness would build the principal chapel, he said, the merchants would then build six more and gradually have all the work carried out. Because of this the Pope changed his mind, although the model had been made and the price agreed; and he went to Montorio and sent for Michelangelo, Vasari, meanwhile, was writing every day to Michelangelo, who sent him news of what was happening. So on 1 August 1550 Michelangelo wrote telling Vasari of the Pope's change of plan, and this is what he said:

My dear Giorgio,
Concerning the new foundations for San Pietro in Montorio, as the Pope did not want to hear about them I did not write to you, knowing that you were already informed by your man here. Now I must tell you the following, namely that yesterday morning after he had gone to Montorio the Pope sent for me. I met him on the bridge when he was on his way back and had a long conversation with him about the tombs you were commissioned to do; and finally, he told me he had determined that he would have them built not on the hill but in the church of the Florentines instead. Then he asked me for my opinion and for a design, and I strongly encouraged him, thinking that in this way the church would be brought to completion. As for the three letters I have received from you, I myself cannot aspire to such heights; but if I were anxious to be in some degree what you say I am, it would be only so that you might have a worthy servant. However, seeing you are a man who brings the dead back to life, I am not at all astonished that you should prolong the life of the living, or rather that you should snatch from the hands of death and immortalize those who are scarcely alive. Such as I am, then, I am all yours. Michelangelo Buonarroti. Rome.

While these matters were being arranged and the Florentines living in Rome were trying to find the money that was needed several difficulties arose, nothing was settled, and enthusiasm began to cool. Meanwhile, Vasari and Ammanati excavated all the marbles at Carrara and they were sent to Rome; and Ammanati went with them, taking a letter to Buonarroti in which Vasari wrote that he should get the Pope to say where he wanted the tomb to go and that, when the order was given, he should prepare the foundation. As soon as Michelangelo received the letter he spoke to his holiness, and then he wrote to Vasari as follows:

My dear Giorgio,
As soon as Bartolommeo arrived here I went to have a word with the Pope; and when I saw that he wanted preparations made at Montorio for the tombs I looked for a mason from St Peter's. Busybody found this out and wanted to send someone to suit himself; and to avoid striving against a man who sets the winds in motion I stood aside, seeing that I'm a lightweight and have no wish to be blown off my feet. Anyhow, I think we have to forget all about the church of the Florentines. Come back soon, and keep well. I have nothing more to say. 13 October 1550.

'Busybody' was Michelangelo's name for the bishop of Forlì, because he meddled in everything. As the Pope's head chamberlain he was in charge of the medals, jewels, cameos, small bronze figures, pictures, and drawings, and he wanted everything to depend on him. Michelangelo tried to keep out of his way, because he found the bishop's meddling always dangerous and feared lest his ambitions should land him in a spot of serious trouble. Anyhow, the Florentines lost an excellent opportunity of building their church and God knows if there will ever be another. This caused me great sorrow; but I thought I should briefly record what happened to show the way Michelangelo always tried to help his own people and friends, and the profession of architecture.
Vasari had scarcely returned to Rome, just before the beginning of

1551, when the Sangallo clique in a plot against Michelangelo persuaded the Pope to summon to a meeting in St Peter's all the builders and overseers, hoping to convince his holiness by slanderous accusations that Michelangelo had ruined the building. Now Michelangelo had built ready for vaulting the hemicycle of the king of France (where the three chapels are) with the three upper windows; but not knowing what was to be done with the vault, and relying on their own poor judgement, they had convinced the elder Cardinal Salviati and Marcello Cervini (who later became Pope) that St Peter's would be left poorly lit. So after they had all assembled the Pope told Michelangelo that the deputies alleged that the hemicycle would have little light. Michelangelo said: 'I would like them to speak for themselves.'

Cardinal Marcello declared: 'Here we are.'

Then Michelangelo said to him: 'My lord, above these windows in the vault, which will be made of travertine, are to go three more.'

' But you never told us that,' the cardinal remarked.

And then Michelangelo announced: 'I'm not and I don't intend to be obliged to discuss with your Eminence or anyone else what I ought or intend to do. Your duty is to collect the money and guard it against thieves, and you must leave the task of designing the building to me.'

Then he turned to the Pope and added: 'Holy Father, you know what my earnings are from this enterprise, and you know that unless my labours bring me spiritual satisfaction I am wasting all my time and work.'

The Pope, who loved him, put his hand on Michelangelo's shoulder and said:

'Both your soul and your body will profit, never fear.'

After he was rid of the others the Pope's love for Michelangelo grew almost boundless; and the following day he ordered him and Vasari to go to the Villa Giulia, where they had many discussions together, which brought that work almost to its present beauty; nor was any aspect of the design planned or carried out without Michelangelo's advice and judgement. The Pope once insisted (this was on one of the many occasions when Michelangelo went to see him with Vasari, and this time they found him in the company of twelve cardinals, by the fountain of the Acqua Vergine), the Pope insisted, I repeat, that Michelangelo should sit by his side, despite his humble resistance, for he always paid the greatest honour to his genius.

His holiness commissioned Michelangelo to make a model for the façade of a palace he wanted to build alongside San Rocco, with the idea of using the mausoleum of Augustus for the remainder of the walls. So Michelangelo produced a design of incomparable richness, variety, and originality, for in everything he did he was in no need of architectural rules, either ancient or modern, being an artist with the power to invent varied and original things as beautiful as those of the past. This model now belongs to Duke Cosimo de' Medici, to whom, when he went to Rome, it was given by Pope Pius IV, and who keeps it among his most precious belongings.

The Pope held Michelangelo in such high regard that he constantly defended him against those cardinals and others who tried to slander him; and he always insisted that other artists, no matter how skilled or distinguished, should wait on Michelangelo at his own house. His holiness held him in such respect and reverence that to avoid wearying him he refrained from asking for many things that Michelangelo, old as he was, would certainly have done.

When Paul III was living Michelangelo had on his orders made a start on rebuilding the bridge of Santa Maria, which had been weakened and ruined by time and the continuous flow of water. He constructed caissons and started to repair and refound the piers, and he succeeded in completing a substantial part of the work, at no little cost in wood and travertine. Then during the reign of Julius III it was proposed at a meeting of papal administrators to finish the work, and it was suggested that the architect Nanni di Baccio Bigio would, by doing it under contract, save a great deal of time and money. They also claimed that it would be to Michelangelo's benefit to relieve him of the task, since he was old and uninterested in it, and that if nothing were done it would never be finished. The Pope was anxious to avoid any strife, and so not realizing what the outcome would be he authorized the clerks to do what they wanted, telling them to treat it as within their competence. Then, without telling Michelangelo, they handed the work over to Nanni, with an unrestricted contract and all the materials. But instead of doing what was necessary to make the foundations secure, Nanni even despoiled the bridge of a good number of the blocks of travertine with which many years before it had been strengthened and paved. He sold the travertine, which had increased the weight and solidity of the bridge, and substituted gravel and similar materials, so that the internal structure appeared sound. On the exterior he constructed parapets and various supports so that it seemed to be totally rebuilt. But, as the bridge had now been thoroughly weakened and debilitated, five years later in 1557 the impetus of the flood that happened that year caused such destruction that there was revealed for all to see the bad judgement of those clerks and the loss that Rome suffered through neglecting the advice of Michelangelo. For he predicted the destruction of the bridge many times to his friends and to me; and I remember his saying, when we were crossing it together on horseback:

'Giorgio, this bridge is shaking. Let's ride faster in case it crashes down while we're on it.'

To return to what we were discussing earlier: after the work at Montorio had been finished, to my great satisfaction, I returned to serve Duke Cosimo in Florence; this was in 1554. Both Michelangelo (whose adversaries tormented him continually in one way or another) and Vasari were grieved at their separation and they wrote to each other every day. In April of the same year Vasari sent Michelangelo the news that his nephew Lionardo had had a son and that in company with many noble ladies they had taken him to be baptized and had revived the name Buonarroto. Michelangelo replied with a letter to Vasari in these words:

My dear Giorgio,
Your letter gave me tremendous pleasure, seeing that you still remember this poor old man and even more because you were present at the triumph you describe, namely the birth of another Buonarroto. I send my heartfelt thanks for this news; however, I disapprove of such pomp, because men should not rejoice when the whole world is weeping. And I consider that Lionardo has no cause to celebrate a birth with the kind of rejoicing that should be reserved for the death of someone who has lived a good life. Now don't be surprised at my not replying immediately; it's just that I don't want to seem like a businessman. As for all the flattering remarks in your letter, I wish I deserved only one of them; and then I believe I could discharge a tiny part of my debt by giving myself to you body and soul. I am constantly aware that I owe you far more than I can repay. Seeing how old I am, I can never expect to square the account in this life but must wait for the next. So I beg you to be patient, and I remain yours. Things here go on as usual.*

During the reign of Paul III, Duke Cosimo had already sent Tribolo to Rome to see if he could persuade Michelangelo to return to Florence and finish the sacristy of San Lorenzo. But Michelangelo pleaded that having grown old he could no longer support the burden of the work, and he gave various excuses for not being able to leave Rome. Finally, Tribolo asked him about the stairway for the library of San Lorenzo, for which Michelangelo had caused many stones to be prepared although there was no model nor any certainty as to its exact form; there were some marks on a pavement and some rough designs in clay, but the true and final plans could not be found.

* The first complete edition in English of Michelangelo's letters (1506–63) was published in 1963 (*The Letters of Michelangelo* translated by E. H. Ramsden, Peter Owen, London).

However, despite all the entreaties made by Tribolo, who invoked the name of the duke, all Michelangelo would say was that he did not remember them.

Vasari was then instructed by Duke Cosimo to write to Michelangelo asking him to reply saying what final form the stairway should have, in the hope that because of his love and friendship for Vasari he would say something that might lead to a solution and to the completion of the work.

So Vasari wrote telling Michelangelo what the duke wanted and adding that he himself would be given the task of executing what was still to be done, and that he would do this with the fidelity and care that, as Michelangelo knew, he was always accustomed to give to work for Michelangelo. So Michelangelo then sent the directions for making the stairway in a letter dated 28 September 1555.

Giorgio, my dear friend,
Concerning the stairway for the library that I've been asked about so much, believe me if I could remember how I planned it I would not need to be asked. A certain staircase comes to my mind just like a dream, but I don't think it can be the same as the one I had in mind originally since it seems so awkward. However, I'll describe it for you: first, it is as if you took a number of oval boxes, each about a span deep but not of the same length or width, and placed the largest down on the paving further from or nearer to the wall with the door, depending on the gradient wanted for the stairs. Then it is as if you placed another box on top of the first, smaller than the first and leaving all round enough space for the foot to ascend; and so on, diminishing and drawing back the steps towards the door, always with enough space to climb; and the last step should be the same size as the opening of the door. And this oval stairway should have two wings, one on either side, following the centre steps but straight instead of oval. The central flight from the beginning of the stairs to half-way up should be reserved for the master. The ends of the two wings should

face the walls and, with the entire staircase, come about three spans from the wall, leaving the lower part of each wall of the ante-room completely unobstructed. I am writing nonsense, but I know you will find something here to your purpose.

At that time Michelangelo also wrote to Vasari that Julius III being dead, and Marcellus elected Pope, the clique that was hostile to him had seized the chance to harass him again. And when the duke heard of this he was so displeased that he made Giorgio write and tell Michelangelo to leave Rome and come to live in Florence, where he wanted nothing from him except occasional advice and plans for his buildings, and where he would receive all he wanted without need-ing to do any work himself. The duke's private secretary, Leonardo Marinozzi, brought Michelangelo further letters from his Excellency and also from Vasari. But then Marcellus died, and when Michel-angelo went to kiss the feet of the newly elected Paul IV he received countless offers; and being anxious to see the finish of St Peter's, to which he believed himself committed, he stayed where he was. Making his excuses, he wrote telling the duke that for the time being he was unable to serve him; he also sent the following letter to Vasari:

My dear Giorgio,
As God is my witness, it was against my will that I was forced to start work on the construction of St Peter's by Pope Paul III ten years ago; and if work on the fabric had continued up to the present time in the way it started, then enough progress would have been made for me to agree to return home, But for lack of money the work has been continually delayed and it is now being held back just as the construction has reached the most exhausting and difficult part. So to abandon it at this stage, would mean the shameful waste of all the labours I have undertaken for the love of God during these ten years. I am writing this speech in reply to your letter, and also because I have had a letter from the duke that has made me astonished that his lord-

ship should condescend to address me so graciously. For this I am deeply grateful to him and to God. I am wandering from the subject because I have lost my memory and my wits, and as writing is not my profession I find it very irksome. In conclusion, to make you understand what would happen if I abandoned the building and left Rome: first, I would make many thieves happy, and I would be responsible for its ruin, and perhaps for closing it down for ever.

And then Michelangelo added in this letter to Giorgio, by way of excuse to the duke, that he had a house and other belongings in Rome, which were worth thousands of crowns, and as well as this like all old men he was in danger of his life because of a disease of the kidneys, colic, and the stone, as could be testified by Master Realdo, his doctor, to whom after God he was grateful for his life. So for all these reasons, he went on, he could not leave Rome; and, indeed, he had no heart for anything except death. In several other letters, now in Vasari's possession, Michelangelo asked him to beg the duke to forgive him, and he also, as I said, wrote to the duke directly. Certainly, had he been up to making the journey he would have set out for Florence without hesitating, and I am sure that he would never have wanted to go back to Rome, he was so moved by the kindness and affection shown him by the duke. Meanwhile, he continued working on various parts of St Peter's, with the object of making it impossible to change what was done.

During this time certain people had informed him that Pope Paul IV was minded to make him alter the façade of the chapel where the Last Judgement is painted since, as the Pope said, the figures there revealed their nakedness too shamelessly. When he heard this, Michelangelo commented: 'Tell the Pope that this is a trivial matter and can easily be arranged; let him set about putting the world to rights, for pictures are soon put right.'

The office of the chancery at Rimini was now taken away from Michelangelo, but he would not discuss this with the Pope, who in fact knew nothing about it. The decision was taken by the Pope's cupbearer, who wanted to have him paid for his work on St Peter's a monthly stipend of a hundred crowns instead; but when the first month's payment was brought to his house, Michelangelo refused to take it. The same year saw the death of Urbino, Michelangelo's servant, or rather, since this was what he had become, his companion. Urbino first came to live with Michelangelo in Florence in 1530, the year of the siege, after his pupil Antonio Mini had gone to France. He proved a devoted servant, and during the twenty-six years that he lived with him he was made a rich man by Michelangelo, who had come to love him so much that, old as he was, when Urbino fell ill he looked after him, sleeping in his clothes at night in order to see to his wants. Vasari wrote to Michelangelo to comfort him after Urbino's death, and he had the following reply:

My dear Giorgio,
I cannot write easily, but I shall say something in answer to your letter. You know that Urbino is dead. I owe the greatest thanks to God, but my loss is heavy and my sorrow is boundless. I owe God many thanks, for while he was alive Urbino showed me how to live and in his death he taught me how to die, not with grief but with desire. I kept him with me for twenty-six years, and I found him a rare and faithful friend; and now that I had made him rich and expected him to be the support and comfort of my old age, he has been taken from me; nor have I any hope left, save to see him in Paradise. God has given me a token of this through the happy death that Urbino made. Even more than dying it grieved him to leave me in this treacherous world with so many troubles, although the better part of me has gone with him. All I have left, indeed, is my infinite distress. I commend myself to you.

In the time of Paul IV Michelangelo was employed on many parts of the fortifications of Rome; in this connexion he also served Salvestro Peruzzi, whom, as said elsewhere, the Pope had commissioned to make the great gate of Castel Sant'Angelo, which is today half-ruined. Michelangelo busied himself with distributing the statues for that work, and examining and correcting the models of the sculptors. At that time the French army approached Rome, leading Michelangelo to fear that he would come to a violent end along with the city. Antonio Franzese of Casteldurante, whom Urbino had left to serve him after he died, determined to flee from Rome, and Michelangelo himself went secretly to the mountains of Spoleto, where he stayed in various hermitages. About then Vasari wrote to him, sending a little work which the Florentine citizen, Carlo Lenzoni, had left at his death to Cosimo Bartoli who was to have it printed and dedicated to Michelangelo. When he received the book from Vasari, Michelangelo wrote as follows:

My dear friend Giorgio,
I have received from you the little book by Cosimo and I am sending with this an acknowledgement which I beg you to give to him with my regards.

During the past few days, although it cost me a great deal of effort and money, I have been happily visiting the hermits in the mountains of Spoleto, and as a result I returned only half-heartedly to Rome, for indeed peace is to be found only in those woods. I have no more to tell you; I am glad you are well and happy, and I commend myself to you. 18 September 1556.*

Michelangelo used to work every day, for recreation, on the block of stone with four figures that we have already mentioned; and at this time he broke it into pieces. He did this either because it was hard and full of emery and the chisel often struck sparks from it, or perhaps because his judgement was so severe that he was never content with anything he did. That this was the case can be proved by the fact that there are few finished statues to be seen of all that he made in the prime of his manhood, and that those he did finish completely were

* In fact, the letter was dated 28 December.

executed when he was young, such as the Bacchus, the Pietà in St Peter's, the giant David at Florence, and the Christ in the Minerva. It would be impossible to add to these or take away a single grain without ruining them. The others, with the exception of Duke Giuliano and Duke Lorenzo, the Night, the Dawn, the Moses, with the other two, which altogether do not amount to eleven, the others, I say, and there were many of them, were all left unfinished. For Michelangelo used to say that if he had had to be satisfied with what he did, then he would have sent out very few statues, or rather none at all. This was because he had so developed his art and judgement that when on revealing one of his figures he saw the slightest error he would abandon it and run to start working on another block, trusting that it would not happen again. He would often say that this was why he had finished so few statues or pictures. Anyhow, he gave the broken Pietà to Francesco Bandini. At that time on the introduction of Francesco Bandini and Donato Giannotti, the Florentine sculptor, Tiberio Calcagni, struck up a close friendship with Michelangelo. And then one day when he was at his house, after they had discussed things together for a long time, Tiberio asked Michelangelo why he had broken the Pietà (which was in the house) and had wasted all his marvellous efforts. Michelangelo answered that the reason for this was the importunity of his servant Urbino who had nagged him every day to finish it; and as well as this a piece had broken off from the arm of the Madonna. And these things, he said, as well as other mishaps including his finding a crack in the marble, had made him so hate the work that he had lost patience and broken it; and he would have smashed it completely had not his servant Antonio persuaded him to give it to someone just as it was. After he heard this, Tiberio spoke to Bandini, who was anxious to have something by Michelangelo, and Bandini then persuaded him to promise two hundred gold crowns to Antonio, if he would beg Michelangelo to allow Tiberio, using Michelangelo's models, to finish the statue for Bandini. This would mean that Michelangelo's labours would not have been thrown away, he said. Michelangelo was happy with this arrangement, and he gave the block to them as a gift. It was immediately carried off and subsequently put together by Tiberio who added God knows how many new pieces. All the same, it still stayed unfinished because of the death of Bandini, of Michelangelo, and of Tiberio. Today it is in the possession of Francesco's son, Pierantonio Bandini, in his villa at Montecavallo.

To return to Michelangelo: it was now necessary for him to find another block of marble, so that he could continue using his chisel every day; so he found a far smaller block containing a Pietà already roughed out and of a very different arrangement.

Meanwhile, there had entered into the service of Paul IV the architect Pirro Ligorio, who was also concerned with the building of St Peter's. Michelangelo was being harassed once again, and they were going about every day saying that he was in his second childhood. Angered by all this, he would willingly have returned to Florence, and when he delayed he was again pressed to do so by Giorgio Vasari in his letters to him. But Michelangelo knew that he was too old, for he had now reached the age of eighty-one. So when at that time he wrote to Vasari by his courier, sending him various religious sonnets, he said to him that he was at the end of his life, that he must take care where he directed his thoughts, that by reading what he wrote Vasari would see he was at his last hour and that the image of death was engraved on his every thought. In one of his letters he said:

God wishes it, Vasari, that I should continue to live in misery for some years. I know that you will tell me that I am a foolish old man to want to write sonnets, but since there are many who say that I am in my second childhood I have wanted to act accordingly. I see from your letter how much you love me, and be sure of this, that I would be glad to lay these tired bones beside those of my father, as you beg me to do. But if I left here I would cause the utter ruin of the building of St Peter's, and this would be a great disgrace and sin. But when the building has been so far advanced that it can never be changed, then I hope to do all you ask, if I am not sinning by keeping frustrated certain gluttons who can't wait for me to leave.

Accompanying this letter was the following sonnet, written in his own hand:

Already now my life has run its course,
And, like a fragile boat on a rough sea,
I reach the place which everyone must cross
And give account of life's activity.

Now I know well it was a fantasy
That made me think art could be made into
An idol or a king. Though all men do
This, they do it half-unwillingly.

The loving thoughts, so happy and so vain,
Are finished now. A double death comes near –
The one is sure, the other is a threat.

Painting and sculpture cannot any more
Quieten the soul that turns to God again
To God who, on the cross, for us was set.★

From this it was seen that Michelangelo was gradually drawing away from the world towards God and casting from himself the cares of art, persecuted as he was by those malignant artists and influenced by some of those who were in charge of the building of St Peter's and who would have liked, as he used to say, to come to blows. On Duke Cosimo's orders, Vasari replied briefly to Michelangelo's letter, encouraging him to return to his home, and sending him a sonnet with rhymes corresponding to those Michelangelo himself had used.

★ Elizabeth Jennings' translation of the sonnet, '*Giunto è gia'l corso della vita mia*'.

Michelangelo would gladly have left Rome, but he had grown so old and feeble that despite his resolve (which I shall mention later) his flesh betrayed his spirit. Now it happened that in June 1557, in the construction of the vault over the chapel of the king (which was in travertine and for which Michelangelo had made a model) an error occurred because Michelangelo was unable to go along and supervise as often as he used to.* What happened was that the master builder shaped the whole vault on one curve, struck from a single centre instead of from several. Writing as a friend and confidant of Vasari's, Michelangelo sent him the plans, with these words at the foot of two of them:

The curve marked on the drawing in red was taken by the master builder as the shape of the whole vault, so that when it became a semi-circle at the apex of the vault he realized he had made an error in the shape of the curve as a whole, as shown here on the drawing in black. With this error, the vault has progressed to the point where it is necessary to remove a large number of stones since it is built of travertine instead of bricks. The diameter of the arch, excluding the surrounding cornice, is twenty-two spans. The mistake arose (even though I made an exact model, as I always do) because in my old age I have not been able to go there all that often. So whereas I expected that the vault would be finished by now, it will take all winter. If people could die of shame and grief I would be dead by now. Please explain to the duke why I am not in Florence.

Then on another of the drawings, showing the plan of the building, Michelangelo wrote:

Giorgio,
So that you can understand the problem of the vaulting better, note the way it rises from ground level and was of necessity divided

* The chapel of the king – *la cappella del re* – refers to the southern hemicycle of the transept of St Peter's.

into three over the lower windows, separated by pilasters, as you see; and they go up pyramidally in the centre, towards the apex of the vault, as do the ends and sides of it. It has to be struck from an infinite number of centres, which keep changing and alter from point to point so that it is impossible to lay down a fixed rule, and the circles and rectangles created by the movements of the planes towards the centre have to be increased and diminished in so many directions at once that it is difficult to find the right way of doing it. All the same they had the model (which I always make) and they ought not to have committed so gross an error as to try and make one single curve of vaulting do for all three vault shells. This was why, to our great shame and loss, it has to be reconstructed, and a great number of stones have been removed. The vault with its ornaments and sections is entirely of travertine, like the lower part of the chapel, and this is something rarely seen in Rome.

When he saw all the obstacles, Duke Cosimo excused Michelangelo from returning to Florence, telling him that his peace of mind and the continuation of St Peter's were of greater importance to him than anything else in the world, and that he was not to worry. In the same letter that I quoted above, Michelangelo asked Vasari to thank the duke for him from the bottom of his heart for all his kindness, and he added: 'God grant that I may be able to serve him with this body of mine.'

For, he went on, his memory and understanding had gone to wait for him elsewhere. (The date of this letter was August 1557.) So Michelangelo was shown that the duke had more regard for his life and honour than for his presence, much as he wanted him at his side. All these things, and many others there is no call to repeat, I learned from letters Michelangelo wrote himself.

In St Peter's Michelangelo had carried forward a great part of the frieze, with its interior windows and paired columns on the outside following the huge round cornice on which the cupola has to be placed. But now little was being done. So bearing in mind his state of health, Michelangelo's closest friends urged him in view of the delay in raising the cupola at least to make a model for it. These were men such as the cardinal of Carpi, Donato Giannotti, Francesco Bandini, Tommaso Cavalieri, and Lottino. Michelangelo let several months go by without making up his mind, but at length he started work and little by little constructed a small model in clay, from which, along with his plans and sections, it would later be possible to make a larger model in wood. He then began to work on the wooden model, which he had constructed in little more than a year by Giovanni Franzese, who put into it great effort and enthusiasm; and he made it so that its small proportions, measured by the old Roman span, corresponded perfectly and exactly to those of the cupola itself. The model was diligently built with columns, bases, capitals, doors, windows, cornices, projections, and every minor detail, as was called for in work of this kind: and certainly in Christian countries, or rather throughout the whole world, there is no grander or more richly ornamented edifice to be found.

And now, having found time to spare to refer to less important things, I must fulfil the useful task and duty of describing the design of the model that would enable the construction of the building and cupola with the form, order and method that Michelangelo had it in mind to give them. As briefly as possible, therefore, I shall give a straight-forward account, so that if it should ever happen (which God forbid) that this work were impeded now that Michelangelo is dead by the envy and ill-will of presumptuous men (as it has been hitherto) these pages of mine, such as they are, may be able to benefit those faithful men who will execute the wishes of this rare artist, and also restrain the ambition of those evil men who might wish to change them. And so this account may please and benefit and at the same time enlighten those men of distinction who are the patrons and friends of architecture.

To make a start, therefore, the model, as designed by Michelangelo, according to the original proportions would show the internal diameter of the cupola at one hundred and eighty-six spans from wall to wall above the great circular travertine cornice.★

This rests on the four great paired pilasters, rising from the ground with their carved Corinthian capitals, and has an architrave, frieze and cornice also in travertine, the cornice going right round the great bays and rising over the four great arches of the church. This is where the cupola starts, rising from a travertine base where there is a platform for walking, six spans across. The base curves round like a well, thirty-three spans and eleven inches thick, eleven spans and ten inches high to its cornice, which in turn is about eight spans, with a projection of six and a half. To ascend the cupola the way in is through this circular base, using four entrances which are over the arches of the bays; and the base is divided into three sections. The innermost section is fifteen spans, the outside section is eleven spans, and the section in the middle measures seven spans eleven inches, giving the total of thirty-three spans, eleven inches. The middle space is hollow and serves as a passage way, its height is twice its breadth, and it is completely covered all the way round by a barrel vault. And in line with the four entrances are eight doors rising in four steps: one goes to the level of the cornice of the first base on the outside, six and a half spans broad, and the other climbs to the inner cornice, which goes round the cupola, and is eight and three quarter spans broad. From the outside and in there is easy access through each stairway to the cupola, with a distance of two hundred and one spans from one of the entrances round to the other, giving for the four segments together eight hundred and four. From here you can climb to where the columns and the pilasters start on a base which provides an interior frieze all the way round for the windows. The frieze is fourteen spans one inch high; and round the outside both above and below there is a small sort of cornice, projecting only ten inches, made wholly of travertine. In the thickness of the third section, above the middle one

★ A span (*palmo*) equals about nine modern or twelve Roman inches.

(which we said was fifteen spans thick) there is a stairway in each quad-
rant, four and a quarter spans wide, divided into two branches rising
one above the other. This leads to the foot of the columns. From this
level, immediately over the basement, there rise eighteen colossal
piers, all in travertine, each adorned with two external columns on the
outside and with internal pilasters, as will be described below, and
with all the space between the piers remaining for where the windows
must go to give light to the cupola.★ The sides of the piers radial to
the centre of the cupola are thirty-six spans, and the facing surfaces are
nineteen and a half spans deep. Each pier has two columns on the
exterior side, the dado at their feet being eight and three quarter
spans wide and one and a half spans high; the lower part is five spans
eight inches broad, and in height . . .† spans eleven inches. The shaft
of the column is forty three and a half spans, the diameter being five
spans six inches at the foot and four spans nine inches at the top. The
Corinthian capital is six and a half spans high, or nine spans with the
moulding. Three quarters of these columns are visible, and the other
quarter is embedded in the pier, accompanied by a half pilaster which
makes an angle on the inside. In the middle of the pier, on the inside,
there is an entrance formed by an arched doorway, five spans wide
and thirteen spans, five inches high; above it is solid wall up to the
capitals of the columns and the pilasters, uniting it with the other two
pilasters, which are similar to those making an angle beside the
columns. These adorn and border the sixteen windows placed all
round the cupola, whose openings are twelve and a half spans wide
and about twenty-two high. The windows are decorated on the
outside by various kinds of architrave, two and three quarter spans
wide, and on the inside they are similarly decorated in various styles
with their triangular and segmental pediments. They are broader
outside and narrower within to capture more light, just as they are
lower on the inside so that they may give more light to the frieze
and the cornice. Each window is set between two pilasters, the same

★ In fact, sixteen not eighteen piers.   † A lucuna in the original.

height as the columns outside. So there are thirty-six columns outside and thirty-six pilasters on the interior. Over the pilasters is the architrave; which is four spans and five 'quarters' high; the frieze, four and a half; and the cornice, four and two thirds, with a projection of five spans. Over this is a balustrade so that one may walk all the way round in safety. And to be able to ascend easily from the level where the columns start, in the same line in the thickness of the shell that is fifteen spans wide, there rises another stairway of the same size with two branches or ascents. This leads up to the very top of the columns, including the capital and architrave, frieze and cornice; and so without interrupting the light from the windows these stairs turn into a spiral stairway of the same size, which goes up to the level where the cupola must start to turn. The design, arrangement and decoration of the base are commodious, strong, durable and rich. It holds up the two vaults of the cupola which turn upon it, and is carefully and skilfully planned and beautifully constructed. So to those who know and understand, nothing could appear more lovely, more splendid and more ingenious. Considering the way in which the stones are bound and joined, the strength and indestructibility of every part of the structure, and the judicious manner in which the rain is run off through numerous hidden channels, for final perfection no other edifice seen or built up to the present time can stand comparison with this great structure. And it is a great loss that those responsible did not do all in their power to ensure before death snatched so rare a man from life that he should see this beautiful and awe-inspiring fabric completed with its dome.

Michelangelo had brought the building thus far and it remains for us only to make a start on vaulting the cupola; and since the model for this exists we shall continue to explain the details left for its construction. He designed the curve of the dome as a three-centred arch in this way:

A.   B.
C.

Point C, which is the lowest, is the point from which he drew the curves of the inner shell of the cupola, so determining the form, height, and width of this vault, which he instructed should be built entirely of herring-bone brickwork, very well baked. He made this shell four and a half spans thick, the same thickness at the base as at the top, and he left a space in the middle (four and a half spans at the foot) which is to serve for the stairway climbing to the lantern, leading from the level of the cornice where the balustrade is. The curve for the interior profile of the outer shell (which must be wider at the foot and narrow at the top) is turned using the point marked B, giving four and a half spans to the base of the outer shell. And the final curve for the exterior of the outer shell (which broadens at the base and narrows at the top) had to be turned from point A. With this arch turned, the void between the shells increases as it goes upwards, taking the stairway which is eight spans high and allows one to walk upright. The thickness of the outer shell gradually diminishes, so that from being, as was said, four and a half spans at the base it becomes three and a half spans at the top. The outer shell is joined to the inner shell with ties and steps in such a way that the one sustains the other. And of the eight sections into which the cupola divides at its base, four resting on the arches are hollow, to reduce the load, while the other four are bound and secured with ties to the piers, so that the structure can last for ever.

The stairs in the middle between the shells are made like this. From the level where the vaulting starts they proceed through each of the four sections, and each rises in two branches, crossing in the form of the letter X, until they arrive at the halfway point of the curve drawn on C, over the vault. The halfway point of the curve having been reached by a straight flight, one stairway thereafter ascends in easy stages round and round and another directly to the eye of the cupola, where the lantern starts. And around the lantern, following the diminished proportions allowed above the piers (as will be described later) there is a smaller range of paired windows and pilasters, similar to those inside.

Immediately over the first great cornice inside the cupola he started to make the internal gores of the vault. These are formed by sixteen projecting ribs. The ribs are as broad at the foot as the two pilasters bordering the windows beneath the vaulting, and they diminish gradually as they rise to the eye of the lantern. At the foot they rest on a pedestal of the same breadth, twelve spans high; and this pedestal rests on the cornice which encircles and leads all round the cupola. Over this in the middle of the gores between the ribs there are eight ovals, each twenty-nine spans high. Above come a series of quadrilateral compartments, broader at the foot and narrowing towards the top, twenty-four spans high. And where the ribs draw together over the rectangles, there are circles fourteen spans high. So there are eight ovals, eight trapezoids and eight circles, each in shallower relief, and providing a marvellously rich background. For Michelangelo designed the ribs and the frames of the ovals, trapezoids and circles to be made in travertine.

It remains to mention the surface and decoration of the curve of the outside of the vault. This rises from a basement twenty-five and a half spans high, on a socle with a projection of two spans. The moulding at the top also projects two spans; and the covering or roof he designed to be covered with the same lead that today covers the roof of old St Peter's. He made sixteen gones starting above and between the paired columns. In the middle of each he made two windows to give light to the central area where the flight of steps climbs between the two shells, and there are thirty-two windows in all. To these he added corbels supporting a segmental pediment from the roof, covered over in such a way that the high new opening was protected from the rain. And springing from right in the middle of the wall between the two columns, over where the cornice finishes, was a rib for each, broader at the base and narrowing towards the top.

Altogether there are sixteen ribs, each five spans wide. In the middle of these was a square channel a span and a half wide, containing a series of rungs about a span high. These made it possible to ascend to the point where the lantern started. They were made of travertine and protected by coffered walls against the bad weather and frost and rain. He designed the lantern to diminish in proportion like all the rest of the structure. The lines were drawn to the circumference so that everything is in exact proportion, and above there is a little temple with round columns in pairs, like those below, and with pilasters on a socle. So one can walk round and see through the windows between the pilasters the inside of the cupola and the church. The architrave, frieze and cornice encircle the top, projecting over the paired columns, immediately over which are various consoles interrupted by several niches, rising together to the end of the lantern, which starts to turn and narrow a third of the way, like a pyramid, till it reaches the final summit where the ball and the cross are to go.

I could have given many more details and particulars, about air-vents made against earthquakes, about gutters, various kinds of lights and other useful features, but I leave them out because the work is not yet finished, and it is enough for me to have touched on the chief aspects of it as best I could. All of it exists and can be seen, and so it is enough to have given a brief sketch, to enlighten those who know nothing about the matter.

Michelangelo completed the model to the immense satisfaction of all his friends and all Rome besides; and he thus settled and established the form of the building. Subsequently, Paul IV died and was succeeded by Pius IV, who while causing the building of the little palace in the wood of the Belvedere to be continued by Pirro Ligorio (who remained architect to the palace) made many generous offers to Michelangelo. He also confirmed in Michelangelo's favour the *motu proprio* concerning the building of St Peter's which he had originally received from Paul III and had renewed by Julius III and Paul IV. He restored to him part of the revenues and allowances taken away by Paul IV, and employed him in many of his building projects. And during his pontificate he had the work on St Peter's pushed forward very vigorously. Michelangelo notably served the Pope in making a design for the tomb of his brother, the marquis of Marignano, which Cavaliere Leone Leoni of Arezzo, a first-class sculptor and a great friend of Michelangelo's, was commissioned to erect in the cathedral of Milan. (And it will be described in the appropriate place.) At that time Leone made a very lifelike portrait of Michelangelo on a medal, on the reverse of which, out of compliment to him, he showed a blind man led by a dog, with the following legend: DOCEBO INIQUOS VIAS TUAS, ET IMPII AD TE CONVERTENTUR.* This so pleased Michelangelo that he presented Leone with several of his drawings and with a model in wax of Hercules crushing Antaeus.

We have no other portraits of Michelangelo save two paintings, one by Bugiardini and the other by Jacopo del Conte, and a bronze relief by Daniele Ricciarello; but many copies have been made of Leone's portrait, and indeed I myself have seen a vast number both in Italy and abroad.

That same year Cardinal Giovanni de' Medici, Duke Cosimo's son, went to Rome to receive the cardinal's hat from Pius IV and, as his friend and servant, Vasari thought that he should accompany him. He went with him very happily and stayed in Rome for about a month to enjoy the company of his dear friend Michelangelo, whom he visited constantly. On the orders of his Excellency, Vasari brought with him the model in wood for the ducal palace in Florence, along with the designs for the new apartments which he himself had built and decorated. Michelangelo wanted to see these models and designs since, being an old man, he could not see the works themselves. The paintings were extensive, varied, and full of diverse inventions and fantasies, showing the castration of Uranus and stories of Saturn, Ops, Ceres, Jove, Juno, and Hercules; each apartment was devoted to histories, in numerous compartments, concerning one of these gods. Similarly, the lower rooms and halls were adorned with stories of all the heroes of the Medici family, starting with Cosimo the Elder and

* I shall teach the wicked your ways, and the impious will be converted to you.

continuing with Lorenzo, Leo X, Clement VII, the Lord Giovanni, Duke Alessandro, and Duke Cosimo. Along with episodes from their lives were shown their portraits with those of their children and of many of the famous people of ancient times, distinguished in affairs of state or warfare or literature, all taken from life. Vasari wrote a dialogue concerning these pictures in which he explained the histories and the meaning of the inventions and the relationship between the fables in the upper rooms and the histories in the lower apartments; and this was read by Annibale Caro to Michelangelo, who derived great pleasure from it. When Vasari has more time, he intends to publish this dialogue.*

In this connexion, when Vasari wanted to start work on the Great Hall he decided that the ceiling should be raised, since it was so low that it stunted the room and robbed it of light. But the duke refused permission, not because he was worried about the cost (as later became clear) but because of the danger of raising the posts by as much as twenty-six feet. However, his Excellency then judiciously decided that Michelangelo should be asked for his opinion. Michelangelo therefore was shown the model for the hall in its original condition and then as it would appear with the beams remade and with a new design for the ceiling and walls, and with the drawings for all the various scenes that were to be painted there. After he had studied all this, and also examined the method to be used for raising the posts and the roof and the steps to be taken to execute all the work swiftly, Michelangelo became a partisan rather than a judge; and when Vasari returned to Florence he carried a letter to the duke in which Michelangelo urged him to carry on with the enterprise which, he added, was truly worthy of him. The same year Duke Cosimo visited Rome with his consort, Duchess Leonora, and immediately he arrived Michelangelo went to see him. After he had welcomed him very affectionately, out of respect for his great talents the duke made Michelangelo sit by his side, and then with much familiarity his

* The *Ragionamenti*, published by Vasari's nephew in 1588.

Excellency discussed with him all the paintings and sculptures he had commissioned at Florence and what he intended to do for the future, and notably the Great Hall. Michelangelo once again encouraged and reassured him about that project, and said that his love for Cosimo made him regret that he was not young enough to serve him himself. During their conversation his Excellency remarked that he had discovered the way to work porphyry; and seeing Michelangelo's disbelief, he later (as I mention in the first chapter of my technical section) sent him a head of Christ executed by the sculptor Francesco del Tadda, which astonished him.★ Michelangelo, to the duke's great satisfaction, visited him several times while he was in Rome, and he also went to see his son, the most illustrious Don Francesco de' Medici, when he visited Rome a little later. He was delighted with Don Francesco, who treated him with great affection and reverence and always held his cap in his hand when talking to him, out of respect for so distinguished a man; and he wrote to Vasari saying that it grieved him that he was weak and indisposed since he would like to have done something for him; instead, he was going about trying to buy some beautiful antique to send to him in Florence.

It was at that time that the Pope asked Michelangelo for a design for the Porta Pia. He made three very beautiful and lavish designs and of these the Pope chose the last costly, which may now be seen constructed and is greatly praised. When he saw that the Pope had it in mind to restore the other gates of Rome as well Michelangelo made still more drawings for him; and he also made one, at the pontiff's request, for the new church of Santa Maria degli Angeli in the Baths of Diocletian, which were to be converted into a place of Christian worship. Michelangelo's design was preferred to many others furnished by various excellent architects, including as it did so many fine and appropriate features for the convenience of the Carthusian friars (who have now brought the work almost to completion) that his

★ The technical section (*teoriche*) is the three-part Introduction to the *Lives*, dealing with Architecture, Sculpture, and Painting.

holiness and all the prelates and nobles of the papal court marvelled at his judgement. His ideas made use of all the skeleton of those baths, out of which was formed a truly beautiful church with an entrance surpassing the expectations of all the architects, who gave him unstinted praise and honour. Michelangelo also designed for his holiness, who wanted it for the new church, a bronze ciborium which has now been executed for the most part by Jacopo Ciciliano, a rare craftsman who was greatly admired by Michelangelo and whose castings are so delicate and smooth that they hardly need polishing.

Several times the Florentines living in Rome discussed how best to make a start on the church of San Giovanni in the Strada Giulia, and at one of their meetings the heads of the wealthiest families among them each promised to contribute to the building according to his means, and a good sum of money was collected. Then, after they had argued whether they should follow the original plans or try to do something better, it was decided to raise a new edifice on the old foundations; and eventually they put three people in charge of the project, namely, Francesco Bandini, Uberto Ubaldini, and Tommaso de' Bardi. They in turn asked Michelangelo for a design, pleading that it was a shame that the Florentines had spent so much money in vain, and adding that if his genius did not avail to finish the work then there was nothing they themselves could do. Michelangelo promised that he would do what they wanted as devotedly as he had ever done anything, both because in his old age he was glad to be occupied with sacred things, redounding to the honour of God, and then because of his love for his country, which had never left him.

At the discussion Michelangelo had with him a young Florentine artist called Tiberio Calcagni who was very anxious to study sculpture and who also, after he had gone to Rome, started to give his time to architecture. Being fond of him, Michelangelo, as was mentioned earlier, had given him to finish the marble Pietà he himself had broken, as well as a bust of Brutus in marble, much larger than lifesize, of which he had executed, using very small gradines, only the head.

This is a work of rare beauty which Michelangelo had copied for Cardinal Ridolfi (at the request of his close friend Donato Giannotti) from a portrait of Brutus cut on a cornelian of great antiquity belonging to Giuliano Cesarino.

So for his architectural work, since his old age meant that he could no longer draw clear lines, Michelangelo made use of Tiberio, who was a modest and well-mannered young man. He wanted to use his services for the church of San Giovanni and he asked him to take the ground-plan of the original foundations. This was brought to him as soon as it was ready; and then, through Tiberio, Michelangelo informed the commissioners (who had not expected him to have anything ready) that he had been working for them; and finally, he showed them the drawings for five beautiful churches which left them amazed. They were reluctant to choose one themselves, as Michelangelo suggested, and they preferred to rely on his judgement; but he insisted that they should make up their own minds and then, unanimously, they picked out the richest. After the choice had been made, Michelangelo told them that if they put the design into execution they would produce a work superior to anything done by either the Greeks or the Romans: words unlike any ever used by him, before or after, for he was a very modest man. At length it was resolved that Michelangelo should supervise the work and that it should be executed by Tiberio; Michelangelo promised to serve them well, and with this arrangement the commissioners were fully content. Tiberio was then given the plan to produce a fair copy, with interior and exterior elevations, as well as a clay model which Michelangelo advised him how to set up. In ten days Tiberio finished a model of eight spans, which pleased the Florentine colony so much that they then had him make a wooden model which is now in the consulate: here is a building as rare in its ornate variety as any church ever seen. But after work had been started and five thousand crowns had been spent, the funds failed, much to Michelangelo's annoyance, and the project has remained suspended ever since.

116

Michelangelo also procured for Tiberio the commission to finish under his direction a chapel for Cardinal Santa Fiore in Santa Maria Maggiore; but this remained unfinished because of the unhappy death of Tiberio himself as well as of the cardinal and Michelangelo.

Michelangelo had been seventeen years in the construction of St Peter's, and several times the superintendents had tried to have his authority taken away from him. When they failed in this they sought to oppose him in every other matter, now on one far-fetched pretext and now on another, in the hope that as he was so old that he could do no more they would force him to retire from sheer weariness. Then it happened that the overseer, Cesare da Casteldurante, died, and for the sake of the building Michelangelo sent there, while he was looking for a suitable successor, Luigi Gaeta, who was too young but very competent. Some of the deputies had often tried to get Nanni di Baccio Bigio put in charge (for he was always urging them and promising the earth) and in order to get their own way the same men sent Luigi Gaeta away. After he had heard of this, in his anger Michelangelo refused to go to St Peter's any more; and they then started to spread it abroad that he was no longer competent and that a replacement must be found; and they also alleged that he had told them he no longer wanted to be troubled with the building. All this came back to Michelangelo who sent Daniele Ricciarelli of Volterra to Bishop Ferratino, one of the commissioners, who had informed Cardinal Carpi that Michelangelo had told one of his servants that he no longer wanted to be troubled with the building. Daniele told him that this was not Michelangelo's wish, and in reply the bishop said that he was sorry Michelangelo had not discussed what was in his mind, but that a replacement was needed and he would have gladly accepted Daniele himself. With this arrangement, Michelangelo showed himself satisfied. However, after he had given the commissioners to understand that they would be offered a replacement of Michelangelo's choice, Ferratino then put forward not Daniele but Nanni Bigio. Then after Bigio had been accepted and installed, not

117

long after he arranged for a scaffolding of beams to be raised from the Pope's stables, on the side of the hill, to the great tribune on that side of the church, because, he argued, too many ropes were being consumed in drawing up the materials and it was better to transport them this way. However, when Michelangelo heard of this, he straight away went to see the Pope, whom he found on the piazza of the Capitol; and when he started to make his protest his holiness took him along to a private room where he said:

Holy Father, the commissioners have found to replace me someone I know nothing about. However, if they and your holiness have decided that I am no longer capable I shall withdraw to Florence where I can stay near the Grand Duke, who has so often desired my presence, and end my life in my own house. So I beg for your kind dismissal.

The Pope was incensed by what he heard and after he had consoled Michelangelo he told him to come back and talk to him the following day at Araceli. Then he called together all the commissioners and demanded to know the reasons for what had happened. They argued that the building was going to ruin and that mistakes were being made in the construction; but knowing that this was untrue, the Pope ordered Agabrio Scierbellone to examine the structure and require Nanni, who was making the accusations, to point out the errors. This was done; Agabrio discovered that the complaints were inspired by envy and were completely unfounded; and Nanni was contemptuously dismissed in the presence of many noblemen. Nanni was also reproached for having ruined the bridge of Santa Maria and, after promising to clean the harbour at Ancona at little cost, having choked it more in one day than the sea did in ten years. This was the end of Nanni's connexion with St Peter's, where, for seventeen years, Michelangelo had devoted himself entirely to settling the essential features of the building so as to frustrate those whose envious hostility made him think they would make changes after his death. Today, in consequence, the building is secure enough to be safely vaulted. Thus we see that God, who looks after good men, favoured Michelangelo during his lifetime and never ceased to protect both him and St Peter's. Then Pius IV, who survived Michelangelo, told the superintendents to alter nothing that Michelangelo had laid down. His successor, Pius V, followed the same policy even more emphatically; and to avoid confusion he told the architects Pirro Ligorio and Jacopo Vignola to follow Michelangelo's designs with unswerving fidelity. Indeed, when Pirro was presumptuous enough to propose several changes he was discharged in disgrace. Pius V was as zealous for the glory of St Peter's as for the Christian religion; so much so that in 1565, when Vasari went to kiss his feet, and again when he was summoned in 1566, he talked only of how to make sure that Michelangelo's designs were followed. Then to avoid any confusion his holiness commanded Vasari to go with his private treasurer, Guglielmo Sangalletti, and on his authority tell Bishop Ferratino, who was supervising the builders, to pay strict attention to all the important memoranda and records that Vasari would give him, so that the words of malignant and presumptuous men would have no power to upset the arrangements or details left to posterity by Michelangelo's genius. Giovanbattista Altoviti, a friend of Vasari and of the arts, was present on this occasion; and after Ferratino had heard what Vasari had to say, he eagerly accepted every available record and promised that everyone, including himself, would without fail observe all Michelangelo's arrangements and designs in the building; he would, he said, protect, safeguard, and maintain the work of the great Michelangelo.

To return to Michelangelo himself: about a year before his death Vasari secretly prevailed on Duke Cosimo de' Medici to persuade the Pope through his ambassador Averardo Serristori that, since Michelangelo was now very feeble, a careful watch should be kept on those who were looking after him, or helping him in his home. Vasari suggested that the Pope should make arrangements so that, in the event of his having an accident, as old men often do, all his clothes, his drawings, cartoons, models, money, and other possessions should be set down in an inventory and placed in safe-keeping for the sake of the work on St Peter's. In this way, if there were anything there concerning St Peter's or the sacristy, library, and façade of San Lorenzo, no one would make off with it, as frequently happens in such cases. In the event, these precautions proved well worth while.

Michelangelo's nephew Lionardo wanted to go to Rome the following Lent, for he guessed that his uncle had now come to the end of his life; and Michelangelo welcomed this suggestion. When, therefore, he fell ill with a slow fever he at once made Daniele write telling Lionardo that he should come. But, despite the attentions of his physician Federigo Donati and of others, his illness grew worse; and so with perfect consciousness he made his will in three sentences, leaving his soul to God, his body to the earth, and his material possessions to his nearest relations. Then he told his friends that as he died they should recall to him the sufferings of Jesus Christ. And so on 17 February, in the year 1563 according to Florentine reckoning (1564 by the Roman) at the twenty-third hour he breathed his last and went to a better life.*

Michelangelo had a strong vocation for the arts on which he laboured, and he succeeded in everything he did, no matter how difficult. For nature gave him a mind that devoted itself eagerly to the great arts of design. And in order to achieve perfection he made endless anatomical studies, dissecting corpses in order to discover the principles of their construction and the concatenation of the bones, muscles, nerves, and veins, and all the various movements and postures of the human body. He studied not only men but animals as well, and especially horses, which he loved to own. Of all these he was anxious to learn the anatomical principles and laws in so far as they concerned his art; and in his works he demonstrated this knowledge so well that those who study nothing else except anatomy

* Michelangelo died on 18 February 1564.

achieve no more. As a result everything he made, whether with the brush or the chisel, defies imitation, and (as has been said) is imbued with such art, grace, and distinctive vitality that, if this can be said without offence, he has surpassed and vanquished the ancients, for the facility with which he achieved difficult effects was so great that they seem to have been created without effort, although anyone who tries to copy his work finds a great deal of effort is needed.

Michelangelo's genius was recognized during his lifetime, not, as happens to so many, only after his death. As we have seen, Julius II, Leo X, Clement VII, Paul III, Julius III, Paul IV, and Pius IV, all these supreme pontiffs, wanted to have him near them at all times; as also, as we know, did Suleiman, emperor of the Turks, Francis of Valois, king of France, the Emperor Charles V, the Signoria of Venice, and lastly, as I related, Duke Cosimo de' Medici, all of whom made him very honourable offers, simply to avail themselves of his great talents. This happens only to men of tremendous worth, like Michelangelo, who, as was clearly recognized, achieved in the three arts a perfect mastery that God has granted no other person, in the ancient or modern world, in all the years that the sun has been spinning round the world. His imagination was so powerful and perfect that he often discarded work in which his hands found it impossible to express his tremendous and awesome ideas; indeed, he has often destroyed his work, and I know for a fact that shortly before he died he burned a large number of his own drawings, sketches, and cartoons so that no one should see the labours he endured and the ways he tested his genius, and lest he should appear less than perfect. I have some examples of his work, found in Florence and placed in my book of drawings; and these not only reveal the greatness of his mind but also show that when he wished to bring forth Minerva from the head of Jove, he had to use Vulcan's hammer: for he used to make his figures the sum of nine, ten, and even twelve 'heads'; in putting them together he strove only to achieve a certain overall harmony of grace, which nature does not present; and he said that one should have compasses in one's eyes, not in one's hands, because the hands execute but it is the eye which judges. He also used this method in architecture.

No one should think it strange that Michelangelo loved solitude, for he was deeply in love with his art, which claims a man with all his thoughts for itself alone. Anyone who wants to devote himself to the study of art must shun the society of others. In fact, a man who gives his time to the problems of art is never alone and never lacks food for thought, and those who attribute an artist's love of solitude to outlandishness and eccentricity are mistaken, seeing that anyone who wants to do good work must rid himself of all cares and burdens: the artist must have time and opportunity for reflection and solitude and concentration. Although all this is true, Michelangelo valued and kept the friendship of many great men and of many talented and learned people, when it was appropriate. Thus, the great Cardinal Ippolito de' Medici loved him dearly, and on one occasion, having heard that a beautiful Arab horse of his had taken Michelangelo's fancy, he sent it to him as a gift, along with ten mules laden with fodder and a groom to look after it; and Michelangelo accepted it with pleasure. Another great friend of his was the illustrious Cardinal Pole, whose goodness and talents Michelangelo especially revered. He could also claim the friendship of Cardinal Farnese and of Santa Croce (who afterwards became Pope Marcellus), of Cardinal Ridolfi, Cardinal Maffeo, Monsignor Bembo, Carpi, and many other cardinals, bishops, and prelates whom there is no need to name. Other friends were Monsignor Claudio Tolomei, the Magnificent Ottaviano de' Medici (a crony of his whose son he held at baptism), Bindo Alroviti (to whom Michelangelo gave the cartoon for the chapel, showing the drunken Noah being mocked by one of his sons while the other two cover up his nakedness), Lorenzo Ridolfi, Annibale Caro, and Giovan Francesco Lottini of Volterra. But infinitely more than any of them Michelangelo loved the young Tommaso de' Cavalieri, a well-born Roman who was intensely interested in the arts. To show Tommaso how to draw Michelangelo made many breathtaking drawings of superb heads, in black and red chalk; and later he drew for him a Ganymede rapt to Heaven by Jove's eagle, a Tityus with the vulture devouring his heart, the chariot of the Sun falling with Phaeton into the Po, and a Bacchanal of children, all of which are outstanding drawings the like of which has never been seen. Michelangelo did a portrait of Tommaso in a life-size cartoon, but neither before nor afterwards did he do any other portrait from life, because he hated drawing any living subject unless it were of exceptional beauty. Because of the great delight that he took in these drawings, Tommaso was subsequently given many others that Michelangelo once did for Fra Sebastiano Viniziano to carry into execution. These were truly miraculous, and Tommaso treasures them as relics, generously making them available to craftsmen. Michelangelo, indeed, always lavished his affection on people of merit, nobility, and worth; for in everything he was a man of judgement and taste. Tommaso also persuaded Michelangelo to execute many drawings for his friends, among others a panel picture of the Annunciation for the Cardinal di Cesis, in a new style, which was later painted by Marcello of Mantua* and placed in the marble chapel built by the cardinal in the church of the Pace at Rome. Another Annunciation, also painted by Marcello, is to be found on a panel in the church of San Giovanni in Laterano; and the drawing for this is in the possession of Duke Cosimo de' Medici, who was given it after Michelangelo's death by his nephew Lionardo Buonarroti and who treasures it as a jewel. His Excellency also has a Christ praying in the Garden and many other drawings, sketches, and cartoons by Michelangelo, along with the statue of Victory with a captive beneath, ten feet in height, and four other captives in the rough which serve to teach us how to carve figures out of marble by a method which leaves no chance of spoiling the stone. This method is as follows: one must take a figure of wax or some other firm material and lay it horizontally in a vessel of water; then, as the water is, of course, flat and level, when the figure is raised little

* Marcello Venusti (1512–79).

123

by little above the surface the more salient parts are revealed first, while the lower parts (on the underside of the figure) remain submerged, until eventually it all comes into view. In the same way figures must be carved out of marble by the chisel; the parts in highest relief must be revealed first and then little by little the lower parts. And this method can be seen to have been followed by Michelangelo in the statues of the prisoners mentioned above, which his Excellency wants to be used as models by his academicians.

Michelangelo loved and enjoyed the company of his fellow craftsmen, such as Jacopo Sansovino, Rosso, Pontormo, Daniele da Volterra and Giorgio Vasari of Arezzo, for whom he did countless acts of kindness. Intending to make use of him some day, Michelangelo caused Vasari to pay attention to architecture, and he was always ready to confer with him and discuss matters of art. Those who assert that Michelangelo would never teach anyone are wrong, because he was always willing to help his close friends and anyone else who asked for advice. (I myself was present on many occasions when this happened, but out of consideration for the deficiencies of others I shall say no more.) To be sure, he was unlucky with the people who went to live with him in his house, but this was because he chanced upon pupils who were hardly capable of following him. For example, his assistant Pietro Urbino of Pistoia was a talented person, but he would never exert himself; Antonio Mini was willing enough, but he was a slow thinker, and when the wax is hard it does not take a good impression; Ascanio dalla Ripa Transone★ worked very hard indeed, but never produced results, either in the form of designs or finished works. Ascanio spent years on a picture for which Michelangelo provided the cartoon, and all in all the high expectations he aroused have gone up in smoke. I remember that Michelangelo, taking pity on Ascanio for his lack of facility, used to help him personally, but it was of little use. If he had found someone suitable, old as he was he would (as he told me more than once) have then made anatomical

★ Ascanio Condivi.

124

studies and commentaries for the benefit of his disciples, for they were often misled. However, he hesitated because of his inability to convey his thoughts, for he was not practised in literary expression, although in his letters he said what he wanted very aptly and concisely and he loved reading the works of our Italian poets. He was especially fond of Dante, whom he greatly admired, and whom he followed in his ideas and inventions, and also of Petrarch, who inspired him to write madrigals and sonnets of great profundity, on which commentaries have been written. Benedetto Varchi, for example, has read before the Florentine Academy an admirable lecture on the sonnet that begins:

> *The marble not yet carved can hold the form*
> *Of every thought the greatest artist has . . .*★

Michelangelo sent any number of his verses to the Marchioness of Pescara, who replied to him in both verse and prose.† She won his devotion because of her accomplishments, and she returned his love; and very often she went from Viterbo to Rome to visit him. For her, Michelangelo designed a Pietà showing Christ in the lap of Our Lady, with two little angels. As well as this admirable work he did an inspired Christ nailed to the cross, with his head uplifted and commending his spirit to the Father, as well as a Christ at the well with the woman of Samaria.

Being a devout Christian, Michelangelo loved reading the Holy Scriptures, and he held in great veneration the works written by Fra Girolamo Savonarola, whom he had heard preaching from the pulpit. He greatly loved human beauty for its use in art; only by copying the human form, and by selecting from what was beautiful the most beautiful, could he achieve perfection. This conviction he held without any lascivious or disgraceful thoughts, as is proved by his very

★ Elizabeth Jennings' translation of:

> *Non ha l'ottimo artista alcun concetto,*
> *Ch'un marmo solo in se non circonscriva . . .*

† Vittoria Colonna (1490–1547), intimate friend of Michelangelo and Castiglione, one of the most famous women of Renaissance Italy.

austere way of life. For example, as a young man he would be so intent on his work that he used to make do with a little bread and wine, and he was still doing the same when he grew old, until the time he painted the Last Judgement in the chapel, when he used to take his refreshment in the evening after the day's work was finished, but always very frugally. Although he became rich he lived like a poor man, and he rarely if ever invited his friends to eat at his table; nor would he ever accept gifts from anyone, because he feared that this would place him under some kind of permanent obligation. This sober way of life kept him very alert and in want of very little sleep, and very often, being unable to rest, he would get up at night and set to work with his chisel, wearing a hat made of thick paper with a candle burning over the middle of his head so that he could see what he was doing and have his hands free. Vasari saw this hat several times, and seeing that Michelangelo used candles made not of wax but of pure goat's tallow, which were first-rate, he once sent him four bundles of these, weighing forty pounds. With all courtesy, Vasari's servant brought these candles to Michelangelo and presented them to him. (This was at the second hour of the night.) And when Michelangelo refused to accept them, the man said:

'Sir, these candles have been breaking my arms between the bridge and here and I've no intention of taking them back. There's a big mound of dirt in front of your door where they'll stand beautifully, and I'll set them all alight for you.'

At this Michelangelo said: 'Just put them down here then. I'm not having you play tricks at my door.'

Michelangelo told me that often when he was young he used to sleep in his clothes, on occasions when he was tired out with work and did not want to take them off just to put them on again. There are some who have taxed him with being miserly, but they are mistaken, for both with works of art and his other property he proved the contrary. As was said, he gave various works to Tommaso de' Cavalieri and Bindo, and drawings of considerable value to Fra

Bastiano; and to Antonio Mini, his disciple, he gave drawings, cartoons, the picture of the Leda, and all the models in wax and clay that he ever made, which, as explained, have been left in France. To Gherardo Perini, a Florentine gentleman who was his great friend, Michelangelo gave three sheets containing drawings of various heads in black chalk, which were truly inspired; after Perini's death these fell into the hands of the most illustrious Don Francesco, prince of Florence, who treasures them as the gems they certainly are. To Bartolommeo Bettini Michelangelo gave a cartoon showing Cupid kissing his mother, Venus, another inspired work which is now in the possession of his heirs at Florence. And for the Marquis del Vasto he made the cartoon of a *Noli me tangere,* another outstanding work. Both these cartoons were beautifully painted by Pontormo, as I have said. Then again Michelangelo gave the two captives to Ruberto Strozzi, and the broken marble Pietà to his servant Antonio and Francesco Bandini. I cannot imagine how anyone can accuse of miserliness a man who gave away so many things for which he could have obtained thousands of crowns. There is no more to be said, save that I know from personal experience that he made many designs and went to see many pictures and buildings without ever demanding payment for his services.

But let us come to the money he possessed. This came not from rents or trade but was earned by the sweat of his brow as a reward for his studies and labours. And can a man be called miserly who helped many poor people, as he did, and who secretly provided dowries for many young girls, and made the fortunes of those who helped and served him in his work? He enriched his assistant Urbino who had served him for so many years, for example, saying to him once: 'If I die, what are you going to do?'

'I'll have to look after someone else,' said Urbino.

'Oh, you poor creature,' Michelangelo replied, 'I'll save you from such misery.'

And then he gave him two thousand crowns in a lump sum, a

gesture to be expected only from Caesars and Popes. As well as this, Michelangelo used to give his nephew three and four thousand crowns at a time; and at the end he left him ten thousand crowns, along with the property at Rome.

Michelangelo enjoyed so profound and retentive a memory that he could accurately recall the works of others after he had seen them and use them for his own purposes so skilfully that scarcely anyone ever remarked it. Nor has he ever repeated himself in his own work, because he remembered everything he did. Once when he was a young man he was with some friends of his, who were painters, and, for the price of a supper, they competed to see who could best draw one of those crude and clumsy figures like the match-stick men that ignorant people scratch on walls. Michelangelo made good use of his memory to recall one of those crude outlines he had seen on a wall, and he drew it as accurately as if he had it before his eyes, and did better than any of the painters. This was especially difficult for a draughtsman of his distinction, accustomed as he was to producing sophisticated work.

Michelangelo rightly scorned those who injured him; but he was never known to harbour a grudge. On the contrary, he was a very patient man, modest in behaviour and prudent and judicious in all he said. His remarks were usually profound, but he was also capable of shrewd and witty pleasantries. Many of the things he said I made a note of, but to save time I shall quote just a few of them.

Once a friend of his started talking to him about death and remarked that it must sadden him to think of it, seeing that he had devoted all his time to art, without any respite. Michelangelo replied that this was not so, because if life was found to be agreeable then so should death, for it came from the hands of the same master. He was once standing by Orsanmichele, where he had stopped to gaze at Donatello's statue of St Mark, and a passer-by asked him what he thought of it. Michelangelo replied that he had never seen a figure which had more the air of a good man than this one, and that if St Mark were such a man, one could believe what he had written. Again, he was once shown a drawing done by a novice whom it was hoped he would take an interest in, and seeking to make excuses for the boy his sponsors said that he had only just started to study the art. Michelangelo merely said: 'That's evident.' He said the same kind of thing to a painter who had produced a mediocre Pietà, remarking that it was indeed a pity to see it.

When he was told that Sebastiano Veniziano was to paint a friar in the chapel of San Pietro in Montorio he commented that this would spoil the place; and when he was asked why, he added that seeing that the friars had ruined the world, which was so big, it was not surprising that they should spoil the chapel, which was so small. A painter once earned a great deal for a work which had cost him a considerable amount of time and effort. When he was asked what he thought of him as an artist, Michelangelo replied: 'So long as he wants to be rich he'll stay poor.'

Once a friend of Michelangelo, who was in holy orders and already saying Mass, came to Rome all decked out like a pilgrim and greeted Michelangelo, who pretended not to recognize him. He was forced to explain who he was; Michelangelo pretended to be astonished at seeing him robed the way he was, and as if congratulating him he exclaimed:

'Oh, you do look fine! It would be good for your soul if you were as good within as you seem on the outside.'

This priest had recommended a friend of his to Michelangelo, who had given him a statue to execute; he then asked Michelangelo to give his friend more work and Michelangelo very good-naturedly did so. However, the friar had asked these favours only because he thought they would be refused, and when the contrary happened he showed his envy. Michelangelo was told about this, and he remarked that he never cared for these gutter-people, meaning that one should have nothing to do with people who have two mouths.

A friend asked Michelangelo his opinion of someone who had imitated in marble several of the most famous antique statues and boasted that his copies were far better than the originals. Michelangelo answered:

'No one who follows others can ever get in front of them, and those who can't do good work on their own account can hardly make good use of what others have done.'

Again, some painter or other had produced a picture in which the best thing was an ox. Michelangelo was asked why the artist had painted the ox more convincingly than the rest, and he replied: 'Every painter does a good self-portrait.'

As he was passing by San Giovanni in Florence, Michelangelo was asked what he thought of Ghiberti's doors; he replied: 'They are so beautiful that they could stand at the entrance of Paradise.'

When he was working for a prince who changed his plans every day and could never make up his mind, Michelangelo said to a friend of his: 'This lord has a mind like a weather-cock; it turns with every wind that touches it.'

He went to see a piece of sculpture that was ready to be put on show, and the sculptor was taking great pains to see that it was in the right light so that it would look its best. Michelangelo said to him: 'Don't take so much trouble; the important thing will be the light on the public square.'

He meant that when an artist's work is put on public view, the people decide whether it is good or bad.

Another time, a great nobleman in Rome took it into his head that he would like to be an architect. He had several niches constructed in which he intended to place various statues, and each niche had a ring at the top and was far too deep for its height. When the statues were put in place the effect was disappointing, and he asked Michelangelo what he should put in their place. Michelangelo replied: 'Hang some bunches of eels on the rings.'

Once, when a gentleman who claimed to understand Vitruvius

and to be a fine critic joined the commissioners of St Peter's, Michelangelo was told: 'You now have someone in charge of the building who has great genius.'

And he answered: 'That is true, but he has no judgement.'

Another time, a painter had executed a scene in which many of the details were copied from other pictures and drawings, and indeed there was nothing original in it. The painting was shown to Michelangelo, and after he had looked at it a close friend of his asked for his opinion.

'He has done well,' Michelangelo commented, 'but at the Day of Judgement when every body takes back its own members, I don't know what that picture will do, because it will have nothing left.'

And this was a warning to artists to practise doing original work.

On his way through Modena, Michelangelo saw many beautiful terracotta figures, coloured to look like marble, which had been executed by the local sculptor, Antonio Begarelli. He thought they were excellent, and seeing that Begarelli did not know how to work in marble he said:

'If that clay were to be changed into marble, so much the worse for the antiques.'

Told that he ought to resent the way Nanni di Baccio Bigio was always trying to compete with him, Michelangelo said: 'Anyone who fights with a good-for-nothing gains nothing.'

A priest, a friend of his, once told him: 'It's a shame you haven't taken a wife and had many sons to whom you could leave all your fine works.'

Michelangelo retorted: 'I've always had only too harassing a wife in this demanding art of mine, and the works I leave behind will be my sons. Even if they are nothing, they will live for a while. It would have been a disaster for Lorenzo Ghiberti if he hadn't made the doors of San Giovanni, seeing that they are still standing whereas his children and grandchildren sold and squandered all he left.'

Once Vasari was sent by Julius III at the first hour of the night to

Michelangelo's house to fetch a design, and he found Michelangelo working on the marble Pietà that he subsequently broke. Recognizing who it was by the knock, Michelangelo left his work and met him with a lamp in his hand. After Vasari had explained what he was after, he sent Urbino upstairs for the drawing and they started to discuss other things. Then Vasari's eyes fell on the leg of the Christ on which Michelangelo was working and making some alterations, and he started to look closer. But to stop Vasari seeing it, Michelangelo let the lamp fall from his hand, and they were left in darkness. Then he called Urbino to fetch a light, and meanwhile coming out from the enclosure where he had been working he said:

'I am so old that death often tugs my cloak for me to go with him. One day my body will fall just like that lamp, and my light will be put out.'

Nevertheless, Michelangelo enjoyed the company of people like Menighelli, a crude and commonplace painter from Valdarno but a very agreeable sort of man. Menighelli used to visit Michelangelo, who once made for him a drawing of St Roche and St Anthony to paint for the country people. Indeed, Michelangelo, whom kings found difficult to handle, would often put other work aside to do simple things just as Menighelli wanted them; and among other things Menighelli got him to make the model of a crucifix, which was extremely beautiful. Menighelli then formed a mould from this and made copies in papier mâché and other materials which he went about the countryside selling. He used to make Michelangelo roar with laughter, especially when he told him some of his anecdotes, such as the story of a peasant who had asked him for a picture of St Francis and was disappointed when he found the robes painted grey since he would have liked something brighter; and when Menighelli put a pluvial of brocade on the saint's back, the peasant was as happy as a lark.

Michelangelo was also fond of the stone-cutter Topolino who imagined he was an expert sculptor but who was in fact very mediocre. Topolino spent many years at the quarries of Carrara, from where he sent marble to Michelangelo; and he never sent a shipment without including three or four figures which he had roughed out himself and which made Michelangelo nearly die of laughter. Eventually, after he had returned from Carrara, Topolino roughed out a marble figure of Mercury and determined to finish it. He had almost done so when he asked Michelangelo to look at it and give his honest opinion.

'You're a fool, Topolino,' Michelangelo said, 'to want to make statues. Don't you see that from his knee to his foot this Mercury is lacking about eight inches, and that you've made him both a dwarf and a cripple?'

'Oh, that's nothing,' said Topolino. 'If that's all, I shall see to it. Leave it to me.'

Michelangelo laughed at the man's naïvety; but after he had left, Topolino took a piece of marble, and having sawn the Mercury in two below the knees and added the length required, he gave the figure a pair of buskins to hide the joins. Then he asked Michelangelo to come and see what he had done; and having had another good laugh, Michelangelo was left marvelling at the way such blunderers, when driven to it, resort to measures beyond even the most competent artists.

While he was finishing the tomb of Julius II in San Pietro in Vincoli, Michelangelo caused a stone-cutter to execute for it an ornamental terminal figure. He guided him by saying: 'Cut away here, make it level there, polish here . . .' until, without realizing what was happening, the man had carved a figure. After it was finished, as the stone-cutter was staring at it in astonishment Michelangelo inquired: 'Well, what do you think?'

'I think it's fine,' he said, 'and I'm grateful to you.'

'Why's that?'

'Because through you I've discovered a talent I never knew I had.'

Now, to be brief, I must record that Michelangelo's constitution was very sound, for he was lean and sinewy and although as a child he had been delicate and as a man he had suffered two serious illnesses he could always endure any fatigue and had no infirmity, save that in his old age he suffered from dysuria and gravel which eventually developed into the stone. For many years he was syringed by the hand of his dear friend, the physician Realdo Colombo, who treated him very devotedly. Michelangelo was of medium height, broad in the shoulders but well proportioned in all the rest of his body. As he grew old he took to wearing buskins of dogskin on his legs, next to the skin; he went for months at a time without taking them off, then when he removed the buskins often his skin came off as well. Over his stockings he wore boots of cordswain, fastened on the inside, as a protection against damp. His face was round, the brow square and lofty, furrowed by seven straight lines, and the temples projected considerably beyond the ears, which were rather large and prominent. His body was in proportion to the face, or perhaps on the large size; his nose was somewhat squashed, having been broken, as I told, by a blow from Torrigiano; his eyes can best be described as being small, the colour of horn, flecked with bluish and yellowish sparks. His eyebrows were sparse, his lips thin (the lower lip being thicker and projecting a little), the chin well formed and well proportioned with the rest, his hair black, but streaked with many white hairs and worn fairly short, as was his beard which was forked and not very thick.

There can be no doubt, as I said at the beginning of his *Life*, that Michelangelo was sent into the world by God as an exemplar for those who practise the arts so that they might learn from his behaviour how to live and from his works how to perform as true and excellent craftsmen. I myself, who must thank God for countless blessings rarely experienced by men of our profession, count among the greatest of them to have been born at a time when Michelangelo was living, and to have been thought worthy to have him for my teacher, and to have enjoyed his intimate friendship, as everyone knows and as the letters he wrote to me can prove. For the sake of the truth and because of the debt I owe to his love and kindness, I have set myself to

134

write many things about him, and all true, which many others have failed to do. The other blessing I have received was something Michelangelo reminded me of when he wrote:

Giorgio, thank God for it, that He had you serve Duke Cosimo, who spares no expense to enable you to build and paint, and so put his ideas and projects into execution; whereas if you consider other artists, whose biographies you have written, they have enjoyed no such encouragement.

Michelangelo was followed to the tomb by a great concourse of artists, friends, and Florentines; and he was honourably buried in the church of Santi Apostoli, in the presence of all Rome. His holiness expressed the intention of having a personal memorial and sepulchre erected for him in St Peter's itself.

Although he travelled with the post, his nephew Lionardo arrived after all was finished. Duke Cosimo had meanwhile resolved to have the man whom he had been unable to honour while he was living brought to Florence after his death and given a noble and costly burial; and after the duke had been told of the happenings in Rome, Michelangelo's body was smuggled out of Rome by some merchants, concealed in a bale so that there should be no tumult to frustrate the duke's plan. Before the corpse arrived, however, Florence received the news of Michelangelo's death and at the request of the acting head of their academy, who at that time was the Reverend Don Vincenzo Borghini, the leading painters, sculptors, and architects assembled together and were reminded that under their rules they were obliged to solemnize the obsequies of all their brother artists. Borghini added that as they had done so with such love and devotion, and to everyone's satisfaction, in the case of Fra Giovann'Agnolo Montorsoli (the first to die after the foundation of the Academy) they could well imagine what they ought to do to honour Buonarroti who had by the artists of Florence unanimously been elected the first academician and the head of them all. To this proposal, the artists responded that, as men who loved and were indebted to the genius of Michelangelo, they must strive in every possible way to pay him the utmost honour. After this resolution had been taken, so that the artists need not be inconvenienced by having to assemble every day, four men of high reputation and proven ability were elected to arrange for the ceremonies and obsequies: namely, Angelo Bronzino and Giorgio Vasari, painters, and Benvenuto Cellini and Bartolommeo Ammanati, sculptors. These artists were chosen to decide among themselves, and in consultation with Borghini, every single detail of the arrangements; and they were empowered to make use of all the resources of the Academy. They accepted this charge all the more readily as they found all the artists, young and old, coming forward eagerly to offer to execute the pictures and statues needed for the ceremonies. They then decided that, in the name of the Academy and confraternity of artists, the consuls and Borghini (by virtue of his official position) should tell the duke what their plans were and ask him for all the help and favours that were needed, and especially for permission to hold the obsequies in San Lorenzo, the church of the most illustrious Medici family, where most of the works that Michelangelo did in Florence are to be found. His Excellency was also to be asked to agree that Benedetto Varchi should compose and read the funeral oration so that Michelangelo's great genius might fittingly be eulogized by Varchi's great eloquence. Varchi needed the duke's agreement to accept this role, as he was in the personal service of his Excellency, but they were certain that he himself would never have refused, being a generous man and greatly devoted to Michelangelo's memory.*

After all this had been agreed and the academicians had dispersed, Borghini wrote to the duke as follows:

The Academy and confraternity of painters and sculptors have resolved, if it please your most illustrious Excellency, to do some

* Benedetto Varchi (1503–65), Florentine historian, who was asked by Cellini (and refused) to correct the style of his *Autobiography*.

honour to the memory of Michelangelo Buonarroti, because of the debt owed to the genius of perhaps the greatest artist that ever lived (one of their own countrymen and so especially dear to them as Florentines) and also because of the benefits the arts have received from his incomparable works and inventions. Thinking themselves obliged to show the greatest possible appreciation of his achievements, they have therefore wanted their wishes expressed to your Excellency by one of their members, and they have rightly asked your Excellency for support. At their request and since it is my duty (for your Excellency was again pleased to have me this year as your representative among them) I have undertaken the task. Certainly, the enterprise seems to me worthy of these upright and accomplished men; and, moreover, I am aware of the way in which your Excellency fosters the arts and (as a unique resource and protection for men of talent at the present time) surpasses even your ancestors, who conferred such extraordinary favours on talented artists. We know that Lorenzo the Magnificent caused a memorial to be put up in the cathedral to Giotto, dead so long before, and had a fine marble sepulchre raised for Fra Filippo Lippi, all at his own expense, and on many different occasions conferred great benefits and honours on other artists. For all these reasons, I have been emboldened to recommend to your Excellency the petition of the Academy, which seeks to honour the genius of Michelangelo, the favoured pupil of the school of Lorenzo the Magnificent. This will be to their great satisfaction and will win the enthusiastic approval of the populace; it will bring no small encouragement to those who practise the arts and will demonstrate to all Italy the magnanimity and goodness of your most illustrious Excellency, whom may God long preserve in happiness, to the advantage of your people and for the benefit of art.

To this letter, the duke replied as follows:

Reverend and well-beloved,
The eagerness which the Academy has shown and is showing in its

preparations to honour the memory of Michelangelo Buonarroti, who has gone to a better life, has greatly consoled us following the loss of that most singular artist. And not only will we give our consent to what has been asked in the memorandum but we shall also arrange for his bones to be brought to Florence, as from what we are told, he himself desired. All this we write to the Academy to encourage its members to honour the achievements of this great man in every possible way. May God keep you in contentment.

The letter, or rather memorandum, mentioned above, which the Academy addressed to the duke, ran as follows:

Most illustrious Excellency,
The Academy and members of the confraternity of design, which was established by the grace and favour of your Excellency, have heard with what concern and zeal you have taken steps through your envoy in Rome to have the body of Michelangelo Buonarroti brought to Florence; having assembled together, they have unanimously resolved to solemnize his obsequies in the best manner possible. Knowing, therefore, that your Excellency was revered by Michelangelo and loved him as much in return, they beg you, of your infinite goodness and liberality, to consent to the following. First, that they may solemnize his obsequies in San Lorenzo, the church built by your ancestors which shelters so many splendid examples of Michelangelo's sculpture and architecture and near which you contemplate the construction of a studio serving the Academy of Design as a permanent centre of studies for architecture, sculpture, and painting. Second, we beg you to commission Benedetto Varchi not only to compose the funeral oration but also to deliver it himself, as he has readily agreed to do, given your consent. In the third place, we beg and beseech you out of the same goodness and liberality to assist the Academy in all that their own limited resources cannot supply for the ceremonies. These things have all been discussed in the presence and with the agreement of the Very Reverend Vincenzo Borg-

hini, prior of the Innocenti, your Excellency's representative at the Academy of Design.

The duke replied to the Academy as follows:

Dear friends,
We are happy to grant all your petitions, such has been the affection we have always felt for Michelangelo's rare genius and that we bear also towards all of your profession. So do not fail to pursue all that you have planned for his obsequies, and we shall not fail to help you in your requirements. Meanwhile we have written to Benedetto Varchi concerning the oration and to the Rector of the hospital concerning other matters that may be needed in this matter. We bid you farewell. From Pisa.*

The letter to Varchi read:

Beloved Benedetto Varchi,
Our devotion to the rare genius of Michelangelo Buonarroti makes us desire to have his memory honoured and celebrated in every way; we shall, therefore, be pleased if you would accept the task of preparing the oration to be given at his obsequies, according to the resolution taken by the deputies of the Academy, and we shall be especially pleased if you would deliver it yourself. We bid you farewell.

Bernardino Grazzini also wrote to the deputies to tell them that the duke was displaying all the enthusiasm that could possibly be hoped for and that they could expect to receive from his Excellency every kind of help and favour. While all these things were being arranged at Florence, Michelangelo's nephew, Lionardo Buonarroti, was in Rome, where he had gone on hearing that his uncle was ill, only to arrive too late, although he travelled with the post. He was told by

* The 'Rector of the hospital' was Vincenzo Borghini, prior of the Innocenti, the Foundling Hospital established early in the fifteenth century.

Daniele da Volterra, who had been a very dear friend of Michelangelo, and by others who had been close to that devout and venerable artist, that Michelangelo had asked and prayed for his body to be taken to his homeland, the noble city of Florence, which he had always loved deeply. So with great determination and promptitude Lionardo secretly smuggled the corpse out of Rome and sent it to Florence in a bale, disguised as a piece of merchandise.

I must emphasize that Michelangelo's last wish confirmed what was certainly true (although many think the contrary), namely, that the reason for his having stayed away from Florence for so long was because of the climate; experience had taught him that the air of Florence, being harsh and raw, was extremely bad for his health, whereas the milder and more temperate climate of Rome kept him in good health, with all his faculties as lively and intact as ever, to nearly his ninetieth year, and enabled him to continue working to the very last.

As Michelangelo's body arrived quickly and unexpectedly at Florence, some of the arrangements for its reception were still to be completed; and at the request of the deputies on the day of its arrival, which was 11 March, a Saturday, the corpse was placed in the vault of the Confraternity of the Assumption, which is beneath the steps at the back of the high altar of San Pietro Maggiore. Nothing more was done that day, and then the next day, which was the second Sunday in Lent, all the painters, sculptors, and architects secretly assembled by the church, where they had taken nothing more than a pall of velvet, richly decorated and embroidered with gold, which they draped over the bier and the coffin, on which there lay a crucifix. Then at nightfall they gathered round the corpse, and the oldest and most distinguished masters each took one of a large number of torches brought for the purpose and the young men raised the bier at the same moment. They did this so eagerly that those who could approach near and get a shoulder under the bier could indeed count themselves fortunate, for they realized that in the future they would be able to boast of having carried the remains of the greatest man their arts had ever known. Inevitably, all the activity around the church had caused a crowd to gather, and it grew larger still after it was revealed that Michelangelo's body was there and was to be carried to Santa Croce. As I said, every precaution had been taken to keep the proceedings secret and prevent the spread of rumours, since it was feared that if a crowd gathered there would be confusion and disorder and also because they were anxious that at that stage everything should be carried out quietly and without pomp, all public display being reserved for a more convenient and appropriate time. However, what with one thing and another, the contrary took place. For as to the crowd, the news passed from mouth to mouth and in the twinkling of an eye the church became so full of people that only with the greatest difficulty was the corpse carried to the sacristy, there to be freed from its wrappings and laid to rest. As for the magnificence of the occasion, although certainly it is very impressive and splendid to see a funeral procession with a sea of wax-lights, a great crowd of priests and sextons, and mourners all clothed in black, none the less, on this occasion just as imposing was the sight of so many distinguished artists, already highly honoured and promising even more for the future, gathered together round the body of Michelangelo to assist in the ceremonies with such love and devotion. To be sure, the number of such artists (and they were all present) has always been very great in Florence, where the arts have always flourished. (And without offence to other cities I think I may say that their first and principal centre is Florence, just as that of the sciences was Athens.)

As well as the craftsmen there were so many citizens following them and so many others who had joined the procession as it went through the streets that the place could hold no more; and, more impressive still, nothing was heard except praise of Michelangelo, everyone agreeing that true genius has so much power that, after hope of further honour or achievement from a great artist has gone, yet for its own sake and merit it continues to be loved and honoured.

For these reasons, the demonstration was more sincere and wonderful than any lavish display with gold and banners could possibly have been. So with its distinguished escort, Michelangelo's body was carried into Santa Croce, where the monks performed the customary services for the dead; and it was then taken (not, as was said, without the greatest difficulty because of the crowds) into the sacristy. Then Vincenzo Borghini, who was there by virtue of his office as the duke's representative, thinking to do something that would please many people and also (as he later confessed) anxious to see in death the man he had never seen while he was living, resolved to have the coffin opened. And then, when that was done, whereas he and all of us who were present were expecting to find that the body was already decomposed and spoilt (since Michelangelo had been dead twenty-five days, and twenty-two in the coffin) on the contrary we found it still perfect in every part and so free from any evil odour that we were tempted to believe that he was merely sunk in a sweet and quiet sleep. Not only were his features exactly the same as when he was alive (although touched with the pallor of death) but his limbs were clean and intact and his face and cheeks felt as if he had died only a few hours before.

After the great crush of people had left, arrangements were made to put the body in a tomb in the church near the altar of the Cavalcanti family, beside the door leading to the cloister of the chapter-house. Meanwhile, word of what was happening spread through the city, and so many young men ran to see the corpse that is was scarcely possible to close the tomb; and if it had been day instead of night-time it would have had to be left open for many hours to satisfy the people. The following morning, when the painters and sculptors were preparing for the ceremony, many of those talented people who have always abounded in Florence attached various verses in Latin and Florentine over the tomb, and this continued for some time; and the compositions which were later published formed only a small proportion of the many that were written.

But to come to the obsequies: these were not solemnized the day after St John's Day, as had been planned, but were postponed until 14 July. The three deputies (the fourth, Benvenuto Cellini, being somewhat indisposed had played no part at all in the matter) chose as their commissary the sculptor Zanobi Lastricati, and decided that they would arrange an imaginative display, worthy of their art, rather than anything that was ostentatious and costly. They all emphasized that it was a question of how a man like Michelangelo should be honoured by men of his own profession whose wealth consisted not in vast possessions but in artistic skill; the answer was to avoid any regal pomp or superfluous vanities, to display ingenious inventions and works full of vigour and charm created by the knowledge and dexterity of our craftsmen, and thus to honour art by art.

So although we had already received from his Excellency all the money we had asked for, and were assured of being given any more that might be needed, none the less we were convinced that we were expected to provide something whose originality and beauty sprang from skill and imagination rather than a lavish display demanding considerable outlays and elaborate equipment. All the same, in the event, the magnificence of the occasion equalled the works that were created by the academicians, and the splendour of the ceremony matched the admirably ingenious and fanciful inventions.

The final arrangements were as follows. In the central nave of San Lorenzo and between the two lateral doors (one leading to the street, the other to the cloister) was erected a rectangular catafalque, fifty-six feet high, twenty-two feet long, and eighteen broad, with a figure of Fame at the top. On the base of the catafalque, four feet from the floor, on the side facing the principal door of the church, were two beautiful recumbent figures of river-gods, namely, the Arno and the Tiber. The Arno was holding a cornucopia of flowers and fruit, to signify the artistic achievements of Florence which have been so great and so many that they have filled the world, and notably the city of Rome, with extraordinary beauty. This thought in turn was aptly represented by the attitude of the figure of Tiber, shown with one arm extended and the hand full of flowers and fruit from the cornucopia opposite; the enjoyment by this figure of the fruits of the Arno also signified that Michelangelo had spent a great many years of his life in Rome, where he created those marvellous works that have astonished the world. The Arno had a lion as its sign, and the Tiber a wolf, with the infants Romulus and Remus; both the river-gods were colossal figures of exceptional grandeur and beauty, and both looked like marble. The Tiber was executed by Giovanni di Benedetto of Castello, a pupil of Bandinelli's, and the Arno by Battista di Benedetto, a pupil of Ammanati's, both excellent young artists of considerable promise.

From this level of the catafalque rose a tier eleven feet high, with mouldings above, below and at the sides and with space for four pictures in the middle. In the first picture (on the same side as the two rivers, and done in chiaroscuro like all the others in this monument) the elder Lorenzo de' Medici was seen in the garden we discussed elsewhere receiving the young Michelangelo, after he had seen in his work some of the first fruits that already promised the rich harvest his great and vigorous talent was subsequently to produce. This was the scene in the first picture, which was painted by Mirabello and by Girolamo del Crocifissaio as he was called, who, being close friends and companions, decided to collaborate in this work. Lorenzo the Magnificent is shown portrayed from life, as with vigorous, spontaneous gestures he graciously receives the young Michelangelo, all full of respect, in his garden and, having questioned him, hands him over to be instructed by some of the artists who were there.

In the second scene which, continuing the same sequence, faced the side door leading to the street, was depicted Pope Clement who, contrary to the popular belief that his holiness had been angry with Michelangelo on account of what happened during the siege of Florence, not only treated him with all possible courtesy and kindness but also commissioned from him the new sacristy and the library of San Lorenzo: places where we have described how brilliantly he worked. So in this picture (painted by Federigo Fiammingo, called Il Paduano, with great dexterity and in a charming style) Michelangelo was depicted showing the plan of the sacristy to the Pope; and behind him, partly by angels and partly by other figures, were carried the models for the library, for the sacristy, and for the statues that stand there today. All this was very well arranged and diligently executed.

In the third picture, situated like the others on the first level, and looking towards the high altar, was a large epitaph in Latin composed by that most learned gentleman Pier Vettori. Its meaning in the Florentine language was as follows:

'The Academy of painters, sculptors and architects with the favour and help of Duke Cosimo de' Medici their head and the chief protector of these arts, admiring the outstanding talent of Michelangelo Buonarroti and as some acknowledgement of the benefits received from his inspired works, has dedicated this memorial, created by their own hands with utter and heart-felt affection, to the achievement and genius of the greatest painter, sculptor and architect that ever was.'

The Latin words were as follows:

Collegium pictorum, statuariorum, architectorum auspicio opeque sibi prompta Cosmi ducis auctoris suorum commodorum, suspiciens singularem virtutem Michaelis Angeli Bonarrotae intelligensque quanto sibi auxilio semper fuerint praeclara ipsius opera, studuit se gratum erga illum ostendere, summum omnium, qui unquam fuerint, P.S.A. ideoque monumentum hoc suis manibus extructum magno animi ardore ipsius memoriae dedicavit.

This epitaph was borne by two little angels, with tearful faces, each of whom was extinguishing a torch, as if to show their grief at the extinction of such a great and rare talent. Then the next picture, facing the door that leads into the cloister, showed when, because of the siege of Florence, Michelangelo built the fortifications of the hill of San Miniato, which were considered truly extraordinary and impregnable; this scene was painted by Lorenzo dello Sciorina, a young man of excellent promise who was a pupil of Bronzino. This lowest part, so to speak the foundation for the whole structure, had a projecting pedestal at each corner, and on each pedestal was a statue larger than life-size with another figure beneath it. These latter were the same size but shown in various fantastic attitudes of defeat and subjection. The first of all these figures, at the right hand towards the high altar, was a slender youth looking marvellously spirited and lively, symbolizing Genius, with two small wings at his temples, as sometimes seen in representations of Mercury; and beneath this young man, made with incredible skill and wearing the ears of an ass, was a splendid figure symbolizing Ignorance, the mortal enemy of Genius. Both of these statues were by the Perugian, Vincenzo Danti; and we shall discuss this young sculptor and his work, which is outstanding among his contemporaries, at greater length elsewhere.

On the other pedestal, which is at the right hand towards the high altar and so faces the new sacristy, was the figure of a woman representing Christian Piety. Being full of all goodness and religion, she is none other than the sum of all the virtues that we Christians call theological and those the pagans knew as the moral virtues. Therefore since on this occasion a Christian man's holy and virtuous way of life was being commemorated by Christians, this figure was given its rightful place of honour, in keeping with the law of God and the salvation of souls; for when Christian Piety is lacking, all the other adornments of soul or body are worth little or nothing. This statue, which was trampling down the prostrate figure of Vice, or Impiety, was by the hand of Valerio Cioli, a young man of fine talent and ability, deservedly praised as a judicious and diligent sculptor. Opposite this on the side of the old sacristy was a similar figure, which had been very judiciously executed and represented the goddess Minerva, or Art. For it can be said, with truth, that after a holy and virtuous life, which among the best men should always be put first, it is art which has bestowed on Michelangelo not only wealth and honour but also such great glory that he can be said to have enjoyed while he was still living the fruits that talented and illustrious men are scarcely able to wrest from fame through their great works even after death. Moreover, we can say that he so completely vanquished envy, that by common consent everyone acknowledged his position of unchallenged and unrivalled excellence. And for this reason, under the feet of the statue of Art was the figure of Envy, shown as a shrivelled and withered old woman, with viperous eyes, whose face and features in short all breathed venom and poison; and in addition she was encircled with snakes and held a viper in her hand. These two statues were by the hand of a man of very few years, called Lazzaro Calamech of Carrara. While still a boy he has already shown evidence in several paintings and statues of a fine and lively talent.

From the hand of Andrea Calamech, the uncle of Lazzaro and a pupil of Amannati, were the two statues on the fourth pedestal, which was opposite the organ and facing the main doors of the church. The first of these represented Study: for those who apply themselves little and slowly can never win the esteem that Michelangelo came to enjoy, seeing that from his early boyhood at fifteen to the time he was ninety as we saw earlier, he never ceased to work. This statue of Study, so appropriate to Michelangelo, was a proud and vigorous youth, who at the end of his arm, just above the wrist, had two small wings which signified swift and constant work; and underneath, as prisoner, was Laziness or Idleness, driven away by Study, in the form of a dull and weary woman, whose every movement was heavy and lethargic. These four figures, arranged in the manner described, made a charming and magnificent composition, and they all seemed to be carved in marble, because the clay was given a white coating which succeeded beautifully.

Another tier arose from where the figures were placed, also square and about eight feet high but narrower and shorter by the extent of the projection and frieze where the figures were. On each side of this there was a picture, about thirteen feet wide and six feet high; and above this there rose a tier similar to the one below, but smaller, with a figure as large as or larger than life on a projecting socle at each corner. These were statues of four women easily recognized from their attributes as Painting, Sculpture, Architecture and Poetry, and included for reasons that were evident in the narration of Michelangelo's life earlier on.

So going from the main door of the church towards the high altar, in the first picture of the second tier of the catafalque (namely, above the scene where, as described, Lorenzo de' Medici is receiving Michelangelo in his garden) to represent Architecture one sees painted in a very fine style Michelangelo standing before Pope Pius IV and holding the model of the stupendous fabric of the dome of St Peter's in Rome. This scene, which was very highly praised, had been executed with marvellous invention and style by the Florentine painter Piero Francia; and the statue or image of Architecture, which was to the left of this scene, was by Giovanni di Benedetto da Castello, who as was said also executed so praiseworthily the Tiber, one of the rivers at the front of the catafalque.

In the second picture, continuing to the right towards the side door that leads outside, for Painting one saw Michelangelo at work on his so highly but never adequately praised picture of the Last Judgement which, indeed, is the perfect model for foreshortenings and all the other problems of the art. This picture, which was executed with considerable grace and diligence by the pupils of Michele di Ridolfi, had likewise at its left, namely at the corner facing the new sacristy, its statue to represent Painting, and this was executed by Battista del Cavaliere, a young man no less remarkable for his sculpture than for his goodness, modesty and perfect behaviour.

In the third picture facing the high altar, namely over the epitaph mentioned above, for Sculpture, Michelangelo was seen talking with a woman who from many indications could be recognized as Sculpture, and who seemed to be consulting with him. Michelangelo had around him some of his outstanding sculptural works, and the woman carried a tablet with these words from Boethius: *Simili sub imagine formans*;* And beside this picture, which was the work of Andrea del Minga, and executed with fine style and imagination, was on the left the statue of Sculpture, which had been extremely well made by the sculptor Antonio di Gino Lorenzi.

In the fourth of these scenes, facing the organ, one saw, for Poetry, Michelangelo wholly absorbed in writing some composition and around him, the nine Muses, exquisitely graceful and each dressed as the poets have described, with Apollo standing in front of them, holding his lyre and wearing a crown of laurel on his brow with another in his hand which he is about to place on the head of Michelangelo. Nearby, to the left of this lovely and beautifully composed scene, painted in such a fine style with such lively gestures and vivacity by Giovanmaria Butteri, was the statue of Poetry, the work of Domenico Poggino, a man who was highly skilled not only in sculpture and in minting beautiful medals and coins, but also in casting bronzes, as well as in writing poetry.

Such, then, was the decoration of the catafalque, which, because it was built with its tiers so diminishing that one could walk around them, was very much like the mausoleum of Augustus in Rome; although perhaps, since it was square, it resembled more the Septizonium of Severus, not the one near to the Capitol, which is commonly called so by mistake, but the true one near the Baths of Antoninus as printed in the *New Rome*.

To this point, then, the catafalque had three levels. The first was where the rivers were lying, the second where the paired figures were placed, and the third where the single figures were standing. And from this last level, there rose a base or socle, two feet high and much less deep and wide than the tier below it. The single figures were seated on its projections, and around it were written the words: *Sic ars*

* Fashioning in the same image.

extollitur arte.★ Then from this base there rose a pyramid eighteen feet high, which had down below on two sides (looking towards the main door and turned towards the high altar) two oval reliefs, showing the head of Michelangelo in a splendid portrait by Santi Buglioni. At the top of the pyramid was a ball in proportion to it, giving the impression that it held the ashes of the man who was being honoured; and above it was a larger than life-size representation of Fame, a figure in imitation marble which seemed to be flying and at the same time sounding the praises and merit of the great Michelangelo with a three-mouthed trumpet. This Fame was by the hand of Zanobi Lastricati who, in addition to his labours as superintendent of the whole work, wanted to show, much to his credit, the skill of his brain and hands. And now, as I said, the height of the catafalque from floor-level to the head of the Fame was fifty-six feet.

Apart from the catafalque, the whole church was draped with hangings of black cloth not, as is customary, round the columns of the nave but all along the chapels; and every single opening between the pilasters, which flank the chapels and correspond to the columns, was decorated by a painting. This produced a beautiful, charming, and ingenious spectacle, and caused simultaneous wonder and delight.

To start at one end, in the opening of the first chapel which is beside the high altar, going towards the old sacristy, was a picture twelve feet high and sixteen feet wide, in which by an original and poetic conceit Michelangelo was shown after his arrival in the Elysian fields. He was in the middle and, on his right hand, larger than life-size, were the most famous and renowned painters and sculptors of the ancient world, each of whom was recognizable by some notable attribute: Praxiteles by the satyr that is in the villa of Pope Julius III, Apelles by the portrait of Alexander the Great, Zeuxis by a small panel showing the grapes which deceived the birds, and Parrhasios with the illusionistic curtain in front of the painting. And in the same way the others were likewise recognizable by other attributes. On the

★ Thus art is extolled by art.

left were those who have distinguished the arts in our own times, from Cimabue to the present day. Giotto, for example, was known by a small panel, on which was seen the portrait of Dante as a young man, in the manner in which he is seen to have been painted by Giotto in Santa Croce; Masaccio by his portrait; Donatello also by his portrait and by his *Zuccone* from the campanile which was next to him; and Filippo Brunelleschi from the picture of his cupola of Santa Maria del Fiore. Then there are the simple portraits of Fra Filippo, Taddeo Gaddi, Paolo Uccello, Montorsoli, Jacopo Pontormo, Francesco Salviati and others, all of whom are full of love and admiration for Michelangelo and greet him as warmly as the artists of the ancient world, in the same way that the poets received Virgil on his return, according to the story of the great poet Dante, from whom came both the idea and also the verse written on a scroll held up by the river Arno, who was lying so beautifully at the feet of Michelangelo: *All admire him, all pay him honour.*★

This picture by Alessandro Allori, pupil of Bronzino, an excellent painter, and a not unworthy disciple and apprentice of such a master, was lavishly praised by all who saw it.

In the opening of the chapel of the Most Blessed Sacrament at the end of the crossing was a picture ten feet long and eight feet high showing all the school of artists around Michelangelo: little children, boys and young men of all ages up to twenty-five were offering to Michelangelo, as if to some sacred and divine person, the first fruits of their labours, namely, paintings, sculptures and designs; he received them courteously and instructed them in matters of art, while they listened to him most attentively and looked at him with truly beautiful and graceful attitudes and expressions. Indeed, the whole composition of this picture could not have been in any way improved, nor could anything more beautiful be desired in any of the figures; and so Pontormo's pupil, Battista, who had executed it, was praised to the skies; and the verses to be read at the foot of the scene ran as follows:

★ Canto IV, *Inferno*.

Tu pater, tu rerum inventor, tu patria nobis
*Suppeditas praecepta, tuis ex, inclyte, chartis.**

Going then from the place where this picture was towards the main door of the church, just at the side before the organ, there was in the chapel opening a picture, twelve feet long and eight feet high, illustrating the tremendous and extraordinary tribute once paid to Michelangelo's rare talent by Pope Julius III, who, wishing to make use of his judgement with respect to certain buildings, had him to himself in his villa, and made him sit beside him. They talked for a good while together, during which time cardinals, bishops and other personages of the court who were present, remained standing on their feet. The composition and the relief of the painting showing this incident, let me say, were so good, and the figures depicted were so lively and convincing that truth to tell it could not have succeeded better if done by an outstanding painter of age and experience. So Jacopo Zucchi, Giorgio Vasari's assistant and pupil, who painted it in a beautiful style, showed that great things could be hoped of him.

Not very far from this on the same side, namely just below the organ, the able Flemish painter, Giovanni Strada, in a picture twelve feet long and eight feet high, had shown when, during the siege of Florence, Michelangelo went to Venice; and there, while he was in the district of that noble city which is called Guidecca, Doge Andrea Gritti and the Signoria sent several gentlemen and others to visit him and make him very great offers. And in expressing this, much to his credit the painter mentioned showed great judgement and understanding, both in the composition as a whole and in every detail; for he displayed inventiveness, draughtmanship and wonderful grace in the living faces and expressions and movements of every figure.

Now approaching the high altar, and turning towards the new

* This is a slightly inaccurate quotation from Lucretius: You are our father, the Discoverer; you bestow on us a father's teachings, and from your writings, illustrious one . . .

sacristy, the first picture, which was in the opening of the first chapel, was by Santi di Tito, a young man of fine judgement and very experienced as a painter in Florence and Rome; and this recorded another remarkable tribute offered to Michelangelo's talent as I believe I mentioned above, by the most illustrious lord Don Francesco de' Medici, prince of Florence. Finding himself in Rome about three years before Michelangelo died, and receiving a visit from him, as soon as Buonarroti entered, the prince rose to his feet, and then, to honour such a great and truly venerable old man with the greatest courtesy a young prince could ever display, he insisted (despite the refusals of Michelangelo, who was most humble) that he should sit in the very chair from which he had just risen; and then he stood and listened to him with the attention and reverence that sons will pay to a good father. At the foot of the prince was a putto, painted with great diligence, holding a *mazzocchio* or ducal cap in his hand, and around them were several soldiers in ancient dress and painted with great liveliness and in a fine style. But, more than all the rest, the prince and Michelangelo were extremely well painted, and very alive and vivacious, so that it really seemed as if the old man was speaking aloud and the young man was listening most attentively.

In another picture, eighteen feet high and twenty-four long, which was opposite the chapel of the Blessed Sacrament, Bernardo Timante Buontalenti, a painter greatly loved and favoured by his illustrious highness, had with marvellous invention depicted the rivers of the three principal parts of the world, as having come, all mournful and grieving, to share the grief of the Arno over their common loss, and to console him. These rivers were the Nile, the Ganges, and the Po. The Nile had as his symbol a crocodile, with a sheaf of corn for the fertility of the country; the Ganges had a griffin and a necklace of precious stones; and the Po a swan and a crown of dark amber. These rivers had been conducted to Tuscany by Fame, seen flying high above, and they stood around the Arno, who was crowned with a cypress wreath and holding in one hand a completely drained vessel and in the other a cypress branch, with a lion underneath. And to show that the soul of Michelangelo had ascended to the state of perfect happiness in heaven, this accomplished painter had simulated in the sky a refulgence which signified the heavenly light towards which the blessed soul was turning in the form of a little angel, with this lyric:

Vivens orbe peto laudibus aethera.★

At the sides and standing on two bases were two figures holding back a curtain, which seemed to reveal behind it the rivers, the soul of Michelangelo, and Fame; and each of the two figures had another beneath it. The one to the right of the rivers, representing Vulcan, was holding a torch; and the figure on whose neck he stood, representing Hatred in an attitude of anguish, and as if struggling to escape from under him, had for his symbol a vulture with this line:

Surgere quid properas, Odium crudele? Iaceto.†

And this was because things that are superhuman and almost divine should on no account be hated or envied. The other figure was Aglaia, one of the three Graces and wife of Vulcan, made to stand for Proportion; and she was holding a lily, because flowers are dedicated to the Graces, and also because the lily is said not to be out of place at funerals. The figure which was lying under her and which was meant for Disproportion had an ape for her symbol, with this line above:

Vivus et extinctus docuit sic sternere turpe.‡

And under the rivers were these two further lines of verse:

Venimus, Arne, tuo confixa vulnere moesta
Flumina, ut ereptum mundo ploremus honorem.§

★ Though living earth-bound, I seek the skies in fame.
† Why haste to rise, cruel Hate? Be still.
‡ In life and death he taught so to spurn dishonour.
§ We are come, Arno, to thy sad waters with thy piercing wound, to mourn the world's glory snatched away.

This picture was very highly regarded, because of its invention, the beauty of the verses, the composition of the entire scene, and the loveliness of the figures. And because, unlike the others, the painter had not been commissioned to honour Michelangelo with his work in this way but had done so spontaneously, with the help that his talent commanded from his kind and worthy friends, he deserves to be commended all the more.

In another picture twelve feet long and eight feet high, near to the side door leading outside, Tommaso da San Friano, a young and very able painter, had depicted Michelangelo before Pope Julius II, as ambassador for his country, sent as we described by Soderini and for the reasons we explained.

Not far from this picture, namely just below the side door leading outside, in another painting of the same size Stefano Pieri, a pupil of Bronzino and a very diligent and studious young man, had shown (as in fact had happened several times not long before in Rome) Michelangelo seated beside the most illustrious Lord Duke Cosimo in a room where they are conversing together, as I explained fully enough earlier on.

Above the black hangings with which, as was said, the whole church was draped all round, where there were no scenes or pictures, there were in each of the openings of the chapels representations of death, or emblems and suchlike things, very out of the ordinary and very attractive and fanciful. Some of the figures of Death, as if grieving at having to deprive the world forcibly of such a man, had these words written on a scroll: *Coegit dura necessitas.*★ And nearby was a globe, which had a lily with three flowers rising from it and was broken in two, after the beautiful idea and invention of the Alessandro Allori mentioned above. There were other Deaths incorporating other kinds of ideas. But among them the one that was highly praised was shown, sprawling on the ground, while Eternity, with one foot on his neck and holding a palm in her hand, regards him with

★ Harsh need compelled.

155

contempt and seems to be saying that neither Death's inevitability nor his will had been able to do anything, for in his despite, Michelangelo lives. The motto read as follows: *Vicit inclita virtus*;* and this invention came from Vasari.

I must not fail to mention that between each of these Deaths was the emblem of Michelangelo, namely three crowns, or rather three circles intersecting in such a way that the circumference of each one passed through the centre of the other two; and this sign was used by Michelangelo, perhaps because he meant that the three professions of sculpture, painting and architecture intersected and were in this way bound together, the one giving to and receiving from the others help and adornment, so that they neither could nor should separate from each other; or else, being a man of high intelligence, he concealed there some other more subtle meaning. But the academicians, regarding him as having been perfect in all three of these professions, and one of them as having assisted and embellished the others, turned the three circles into three intertwined crowns with the motto: *Tergeminis tollit honoribus*; meaning by this that in all three professions he rightly merited the crown of utter perfection.

On the pulpit, where Varchi made the funeral oration, which was afterwards printed, there was no ornament at all; for since it was bronze and decorated with scenes in half and low relief by the great Donatello, any adornment that might have been added would have been far inferior. But on the other pulpit opposite, which is not raised on its columns, there was a picture eight feet high and just over four feet long, of good invention and excellent design, showing a Fame, or Honour, a young man in a very beautiful attitude, with a trumpet in the right hand and with the feet resting on Time and Death, to demonstrate that fame and honour, despite death and time, preserve in eternal life those whose work has been outstanding in this life. And this picture was from the hand of Vincenzo Danti, a Perugian sculptor, of whom I have spoken and will say more elsewhere.

* Glorious virtue conquered.

Having been furnished in this way and adorned with lights, the church became crowded by people beyond number, for everyone, putting every other care aside, had run to see this noble spectacle. When the procession entered the church, first came the duke's representative, accompanied by the captain and halbardiers of the duke's guard, and followed by the consuls and the academicians, and, in brief, by all the painters, sculptors, and architects of Florence. After all these had taken their places between the catafalque and the high altar, where for a good space of time they had been awaited by a vast gathering of nobles and gentlemen, seated according to their personal rank, a solemn Mass for the Dead was begun, with music and every kind of ceremony. After Mass finished, Varchi mounted the pulpit to perform an office which he had not undertaken since the death of Duke Cosimo's daughter, the most illustrious duchess of Ferrara. Then with the elegance of manner, the expressions, and the tone of voice which were peculiarly characteristic of his style of oratory, Varchi praised the divine Michelangelo, describing his merits, his life, and his works. One can truthfully say that Michelangelo was most fortunate not to have died before our Academy was established, considering the magnificent pomp and ceremony with which it honoured his death. And it must be counted fortunate that he passed on to everlasting life and happiness before Varchi, for he could not have been eulogized by a more eloquent or learned man. Benedetto Varchi's funeral oration was published fairly soon afterwards, as was another very fine oration, praising Michelangelo and the art of painting, which was composed by the most noble and learned Leonardo Salviati, who was then a young man of about twenty-two, a brilliantly accomplished and versatile writer, in both Latin and Tuscan, as is recognized today and as the whole world will discover in the future.

But what shall I say, or what can I say that will be adequate, of the ability, goodness, and foresight shown by the Very Reverend Vincenzo Borghini? Let it be enough to record that it was with

Borghini as their leader, guide, and counsellor that the accomplished artists of the Academy of Design solemnized Michelangelo's obsequies. For although each artist was capable of achieving far more in his own branch of art than was required for the obsequies, on this occasion, as always when an enterprise is to be carried through worthily, it was necessary to put a single man with complete authority in charge of all the arrangements. As it was not possible in a single day for the whole city to see the decorations in Santa Croce (as the duke wished) everything was left standing for several weeks, to the satisfaction of the people of Florence and of visiting strangers from places around.

Now I shall not include here the very many epitaphs and verses in Latin and Tuscan composed by various able men in honour of Michelangelo, for they would need a volume to themselves and in any case have been quoted and published elsewhere. But I shall not omit to mention, as I end this *Life*, that after Michelangelo had been honoured in all the ways described above, the duke then ordered that he should be entombed in Santa Croce, where he had himself expressed the wish to be buried along with his ancestors. To Michelangelo's nephew Lionardo, his Excellency gave all the marbles and variegated stones that were needed for the sepulchre, which was designed by Giorgio Vasari and carried out by Battista Lorenzi, an able sculptor, who also did the bust of Michelangelo. Three statues, representing Painting, Sculpture, and Architecture, are to adorn the tomb; and these have been allocated to Battista, to Giovanni dell'Opera, and to Valerio Cioli, Florentine sculptors. Work on the statues and the tomb is proceeding now and they will soon be finished and put in place. The cost of the tomb (not counting the marbles received from the duke) is being met by Lionardo Buonarroti; but in order not to fail in any way in honouring the memory of the great Michelangelo, his Excellency proposes to place his bust with a memorial tablet in the cathedral, where are to be found the busts and names of other distinguished Florentines.

Plates

PLATE I

The Battle of the Centaurs

Marble relief, Florence, Casa Buonarroti

It was at this time [before 1492] that, with advice from Politian, a distinguished man of letters, Michelangelo carved from a piece of marble given him by Lorenzo the Battle of Hercules with the Centaurs. (p. 22)

This very early work shows Michelangelo experimenting with the deeply undercut style of ancient Roman Battle Sarcophagi, quite different from the very shallow relief used by Donatello which he imitated in the next work mentioned by Vasari.

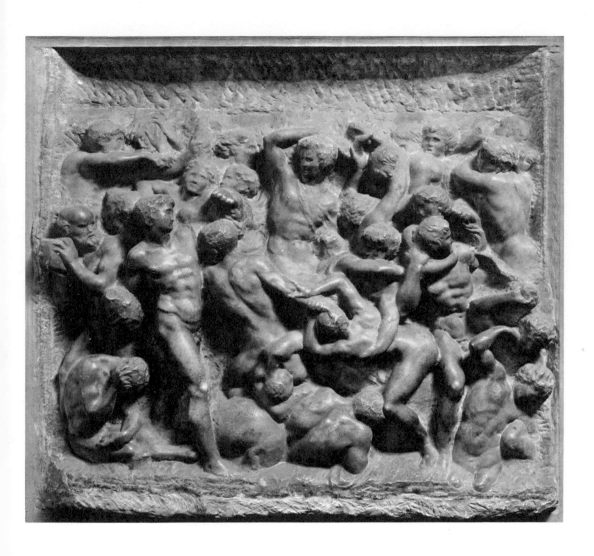

PLATE 2

Drawing after a lost fresco by Masaccio

Pen and ink, Vienna, Albertina

He spent many months in the church of the Carmine making draw-ings from the pictures by Masaccio: he copied these with such judge-ment that the craftsmen and all the others who saw his work were astonished . . . (p. 22)

Vasari's statement is confirmed by the existence of a small number of drawings after Giotto and Masaccio, which are clearly early works by Michelangelo. This pen drawing preserves for us a part of a fresco by Masaccio, representing the Consecration of the Carmine, *which is described by Vasari in his* Life of Masaccio. *It was destroyed about 1600. The drawing dates from about 1491–2 and confirms Michelangelo's study of the works of his great pre-decessors rather than his immediate elders such as Ghirlandaio.*

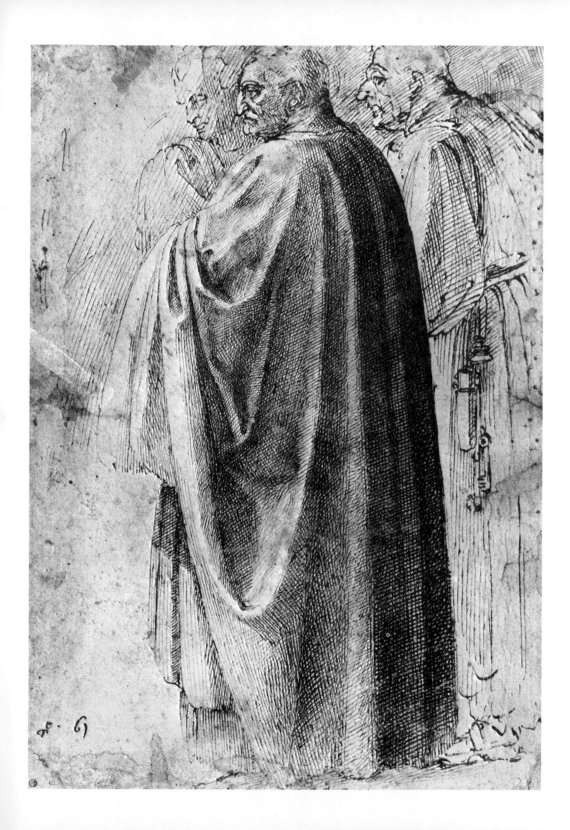

PLATE 3

Crucifix from Santo Spirito, Florence

Poplar-wood, Florence, Casa Buonarroti

For the church of Santo Spirito in Florence Michelangelo made a crucifix of wood which was placed above the lunette of the high altar, where it still is. (p. 23)

This crucifix was discovered in Santo Spirito in 1963 by Dr. M. Lisner, and her attribution of it to Michelangelo has now been accepted by several other scholars.

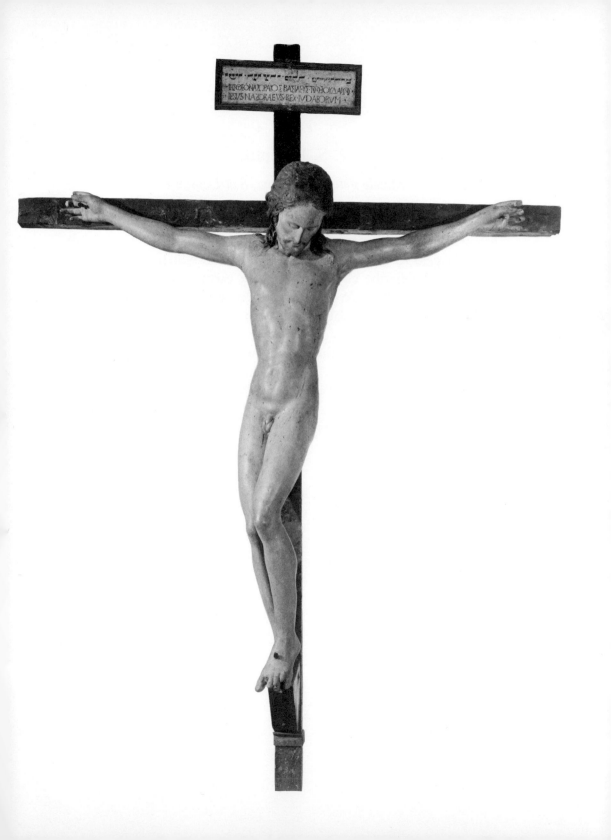

PLATE 4

S. Proculus

Marble statuette, Bologna, San Domenico

. . . a few weeks before the Medici were driven out of Florence
Michelangelo had left for Bologna. . . . One day Aldovrandi took
Michelangelo to see the tomb of St. Dominic which had been ex-
ecuted (as I describe elsewhere) by the early sculptors, Giovanni
Pisano and, later, Niccolò dell' Arca. There were two figures missing:
an angel holding a candelabrum and a St. Petronius, both about two
feet high. . . . Michelangelo . . . executed the two figures . . .
Michelangelo stayed in Bologna just over a year . . . (pp. 23–4)

*This statuette represents St. Proculus, not St. Petronius, but it is generally
agreed to be the finer of the two and is mentioned as Michelangelo's work by
Leandro Alberti as early as 1535. The year spent by Michelangelo in Bologna
was 1494–5.*

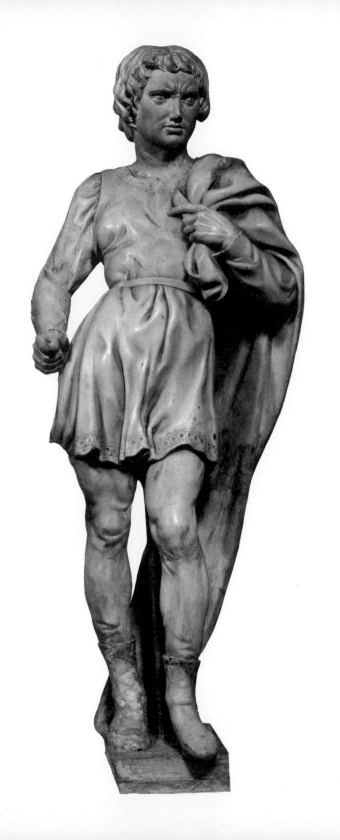

PLATE 5

Bacchus

Marble, Florence, Museo Nazionale del Bargello

Michelangelo's abilities were then clearly recognized by a Roman gentleman called Jacopo Galli, and this discerning person commissioned from him a marble life-sized statue of Cupid and then a Bacchus, ten spans high, holding a cup in his right hand and the skin of a tiger in his left, with a bunch of grapes which a little satyr is trying to nibble. In this figure it is clear that Michelangelo wanted to obtain a marvellous harmony of various elements, notably in giving it the slenderness of a youth combined with the fullness and roundness of the female form. (p. 26)

This statue was carved in 1496, during Michelangelo's first Roman visit, and the naturalism of the drunken stagger and unfocussed eyes undoubtedly increased his reputation among contemporaries, although later critics have found such realism unpleasing.

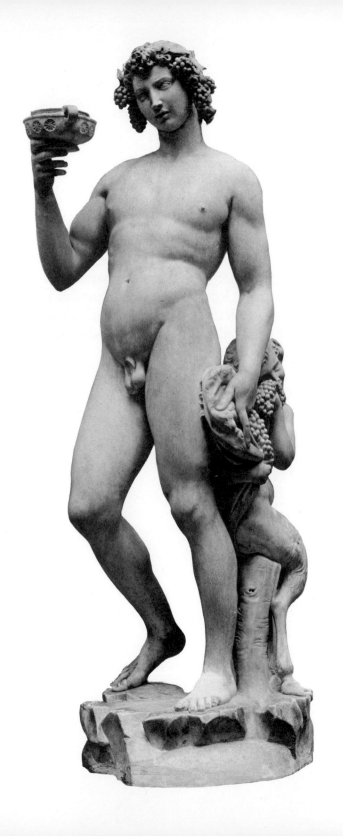

PLATE 6

Pietà

Marble, Rome, St. Peter's

The French Cardinal of Saint-Denis . . . commissioned Michel-angelo to make a Pietà of marble in the round. . . . The Pietà was a revelation of all the potentialities and force of the art of sculpture. . . . The lovely expression of the head, the harmony in the joints and attachments of the arms, legs, and trunk, and the fine tracery of pulses and veins are all so wonderful that it staggers belief that the hand of an artist could have executed this inspired and admirable work so per-fectly and in so short a time. (pp. 26–7)

This, the last statue by Michelangelo in which the marble has been highly polished, was commissioned in 1498 for Old St. Peter's, and was finished about 1500. The composition, linking the two figures into a single pyramidal shape, is not common in Italy and was probably derived from earlier German types, which, however, place far more emphasis on the sufferings of Christ.

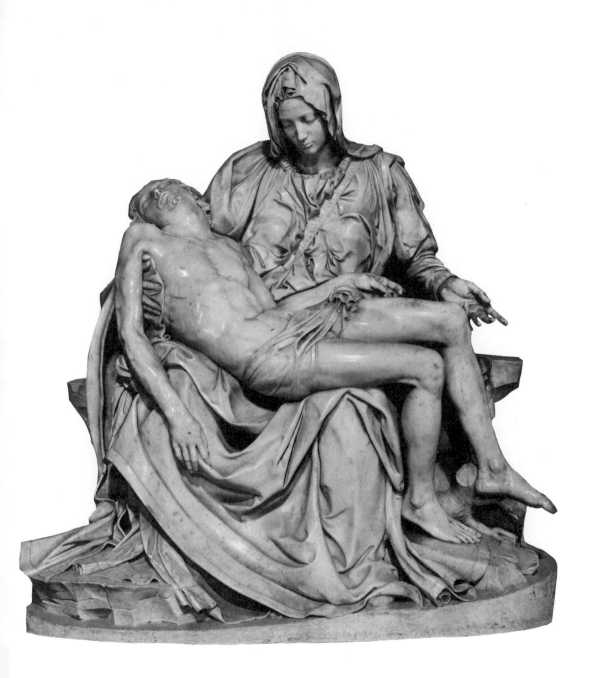

PLATE 7

Detail of the head of the Virgin from the Pietà

Marble, Rome, St. Peter's

There are some critics, more or less fools, who say that he made Our Lady look too young. They fail to see that those who keep their virginity unspotted stay for a long time fresh and youthful, just as those afflicted as Christ was do the opposite. (p. 28)

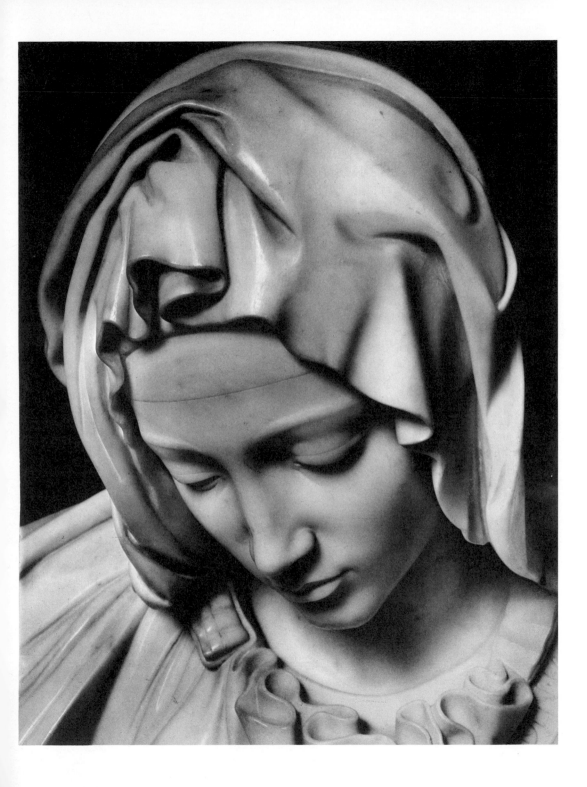

PLATE 8

Detail of the head of David

Colossal marble statue, Florence, Accademia

Without any doubt this figure has put in the shade every other statue, ancient or modern, Greek or Roman. Neither the Marforio in Rome, nor the Tiber and the Nile of the Belvedere, nor the colossal statues of Monte Cavallo can be compared with Michelangelo's David . . . The David was put in position in the year 1504. It established Michelangelo's reputation as a sculptor . . . (p. 30)

It is interesting that Vasari compares this colossal figure—more than 17 feet high—to some rather undistinguished antique statues of colossal proportions, rather than with the Apollo Belvedere, rediscovered in Rome a few years before Michelangelo completed his David. There can be no doubt that this was the first large nude statue in the round since classical times, in which the problems of anatomy and proportion have been solved apparently without effort.

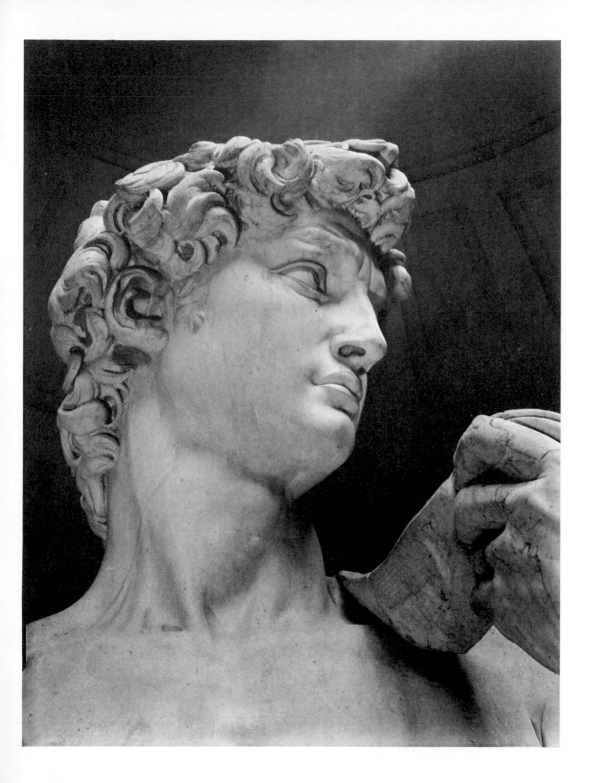

PLATE 9

The Taddei Tondo

Marble relief, London, Royal Academy of Arts

At this time [about 1504] Michelangelo also blocked out (without ever finishing) two marble roundels, one for Taddeo Taddei (which is to be found in his house today) and the other for Bartolommeo Pitti. (pp. 30–1)

See comment on plate 11

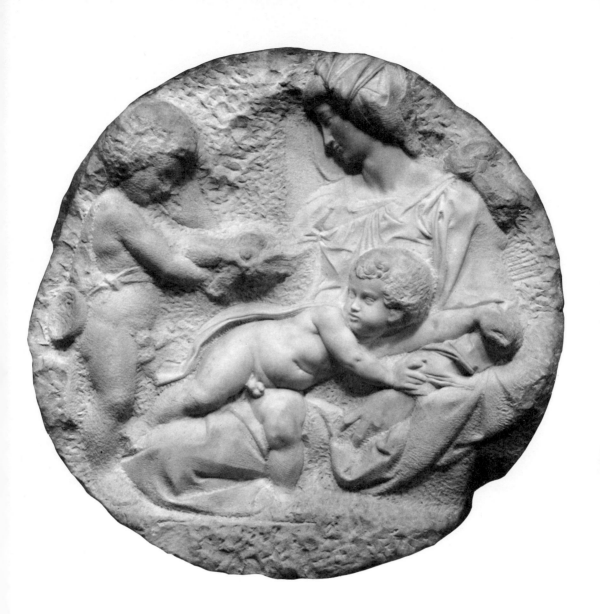

PLATE 10

Madonna and Child

Marble, Bruges, Saint-Sauveur

Michelangelo also made a bronze tondo of Our Lady which he cast at the request of certain Flemish merchants of the Mouscron family, men of great distinction in their own country, who paid him a hundred crowns and sent the work to Bruges. (p. 31)

The marble statue of the Madonna and Child in Bruges is usually identified with Vasari's 'bronze tondo' since it seems unlikely that Michelangelo made two separate works, both of which went to Bruges, at about the same time. The mention in Vasari is in the context of the David *and the* Doni Tondo, *i.e. about 1504, which fits the style of the Bruges Madonna. Vasari probably never saw this work, since it went straight to Flanders before he was born, and it seems to have been practically unknown in Italy. Even Condivi, who wrote more or less under Michelangelo's supervision, describes the work as in bronze.*

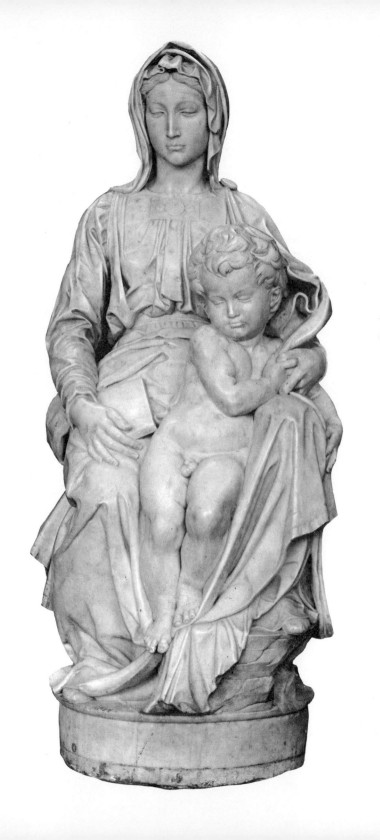

PLATE 11

The Doni Tondo

Tempera on panel, Florence, Uffizi

Then Angelo Doni, a Florentine who loved to own beautiful things by ancient or modern artists, decided he would like his friend to make something for him. So Michelangelo started work on a round painting of the Madonna. This picture shows Our Lady kneeling down and holding out the child to St Joseph. . . . Not content with this achievement, to show his superb mastery of painting, Michelangelo depicted in the background several nude figures, some leaning, others standing and seated . . . (p. 31)

The Doni tondo and the Taddei tondo (plate 9) together with the other marble tondo (now in the Bargello, Florence) show Michelangelo's interest in the problems of grouping a child with one or more adults in a composition that could be contained within a circle. The nude figures in the background of the Doni tondo have never been satisfactorily explained, but they relate formally to the Ignudi *of the Sistine Ceiling and the lost Cascina cartoon.*

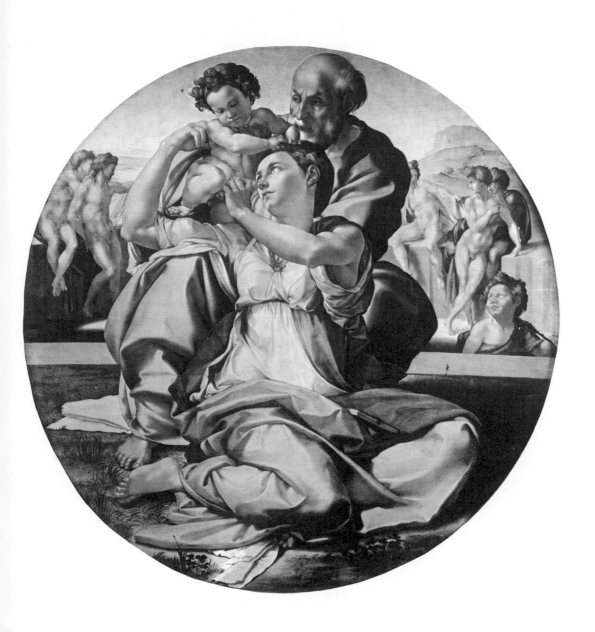

PLATE 12

Study for one of the figures in the Cascina Cartoon

Black chalk heightened with white, Vienna, Albertina

He started work on a vast cartoon which he refused to let anyone see. He filled it with naked men who are bathing because of the heat. . . . There were also many groups of figures drawn in different ways: some outlined in charcoal, others sketched with a few strokes, some shaded gradually and heightened with lead–white . . . (pp. 32–3)

This is one of a small number of drawings which may be considered as studies by Michelangelo from the model for his cartoon. The actual cartoon was being worked on in the winter of 1504–5, but it was destroyed in the 16th century and is known to us only from a partial copy by Aristotile da Sangallo (in the collection of Lord Leicester at Holkham Hall) and from studies such as this, which can be related to the copy. This chalk drawing is not accepted by all authorities as being entirely by Michelangelo, and it is thought that it may have been touched up by a later hand.

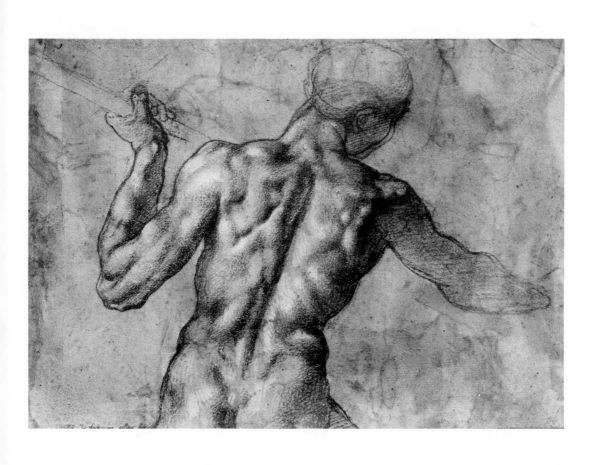

PLATE 13

Moses

Colossal marble statue, Rome, S. Pietro in Vincoli

Of this work [the projected Tomb of Pope Julius II] Michelangelo executed during the lifetime and after the death of Julius four statues completed, and eight which were only blocked out. . . . On the corners of the first cornice were to go four large figures, representing the Active and the Contemplative Life, St. Paul and Moses. . . . Michelangelo also finished the Moses, a beautiful statue in marble ten feet high. With this no other modern work will ever bear comparison (nor, indeed, do the statues of the ancient world) . . . and subsequently . . . one of the shorter sides was erected in San Pietro in Vincoli. (pp. 34–7)

Michelangelo himself thought of the grandiose project for the Tomb of Julius II as the tragedy of his life. After many years of wasted labour and argument, all that was erected in San Pietro in Vincoli was a mere shadow of the tomb originally planned for St. Peter's itself. The work was begun in 1505 and the Moses figure was carved as part of the revised contract of 1513 and finally erected in 1545.

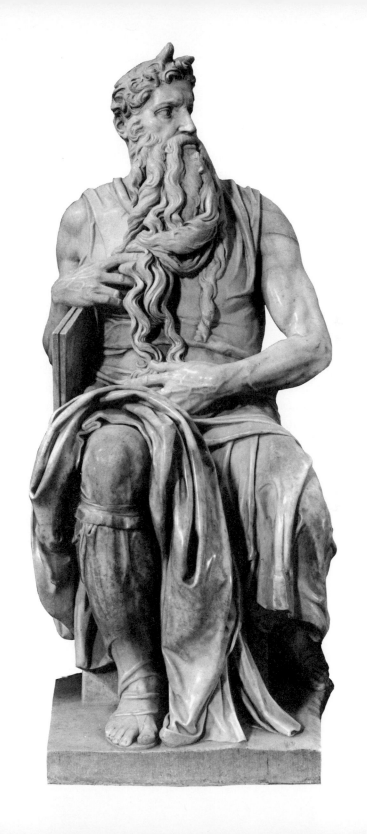

PLATE 14

Sistine Chapel Ceiling and the Last Judgement

Fresco, Rome, Vatican

Eventually they [Bramante and Raphael] persuaded his holiness to get Michelangelo on his return to paint, as a memorial for his uncle Sixtus, the ceiling of the chapel that he had built in the Vatican. . . . So when Michelangelo returned to Rome he found the Pope resolved to leave the tomb as it was for the time being, and he was told to paint the ceiling of the chapel. . . . But the more he refused, the more determined he made the Pope . . . (pp. 41–2)

At that very time the Pope took it into his head to have him near him in person, as he wanted to have painted the walls of the Sistine Chapel, where Michelangelo had painted the ceiling for Julius II, who was the nephew of Sixtus. On the principal wall behind the altar, Clement wanted him to paint the Last Judgement, and he was determined that it should be a masterpiece . . . (p. 67)

The Sistine ceiling was painted between 1508 and 1512, and the Last Judgement *between 1536 and 1541.*

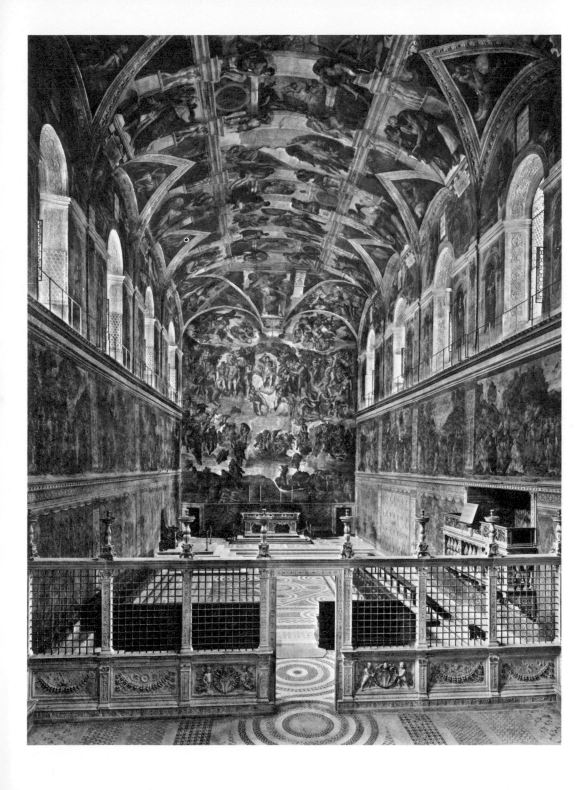

PLATE 15

The Creation of Adam, detail from the Sistine Chapel ceiling

Fresco, Rome, Vatican

. . . and this effect is achieved by the venerable majesty of the Divine Form and the way in which he moves, embracing some of the *putti* with one arm, as if to support himself, while with the other he stretches out his right hand towards Adam, a figure whose beauty, pose, and contours are such that it seems to have been fashioned that very moment by the first and supreme creator rather than by the drawing and brush of a mortal man. (p. 48)

See comment on plate 16

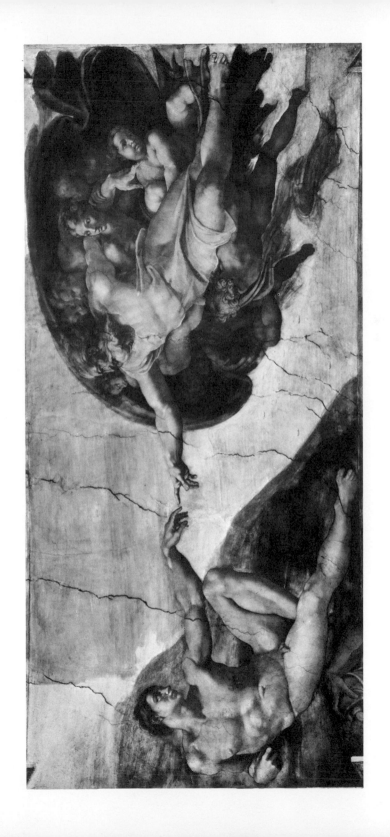

PLATE 16

Adam

Red chalk, London, British Museum

The fresco (plate 15) was painted after 1511, during the second phase (1511–12) of execution of the Sistine ceiling. The most interesting feature of the drawing is the extreme care with which the anatomy is rendered, so that Michelangelo had an exact study from which he could, as the fresco shows, make generalized and stylized statements about the ideal form of the male nude.

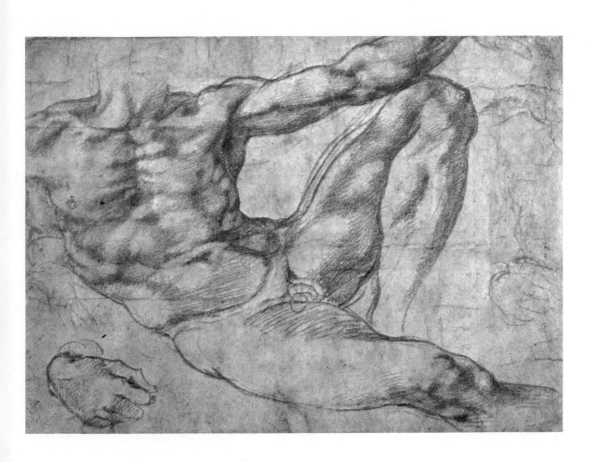

PLATE 17

Jonah, detail from the Sistine Chapel ceiling

Fresco, Rome, Vatican

Then who is not filled with admiration and amazement at the awesome sight of Jonah, the last figure in the chapel? The vaulting naturally springs forward, following the curve of the masonry; but through the force of art it is apparently straightened out by the figure of Jonah, which bends in the opposite direction; and thus vanquished by the art of design, with its lights and shades, the ceiling even appears to recede. (pp. 52–3)

The extraordinary virtuosity of this foreshortened figure has always attracted comment, and it is one of the aspects of Michelangelo's art which most appealed to the Mannerists. In their enthusiasm for contrapposto *poses of this kind they forgot that Michelangelo was here expressing the idea of Jonah as an Old Testament precursor of the Resurrection.*

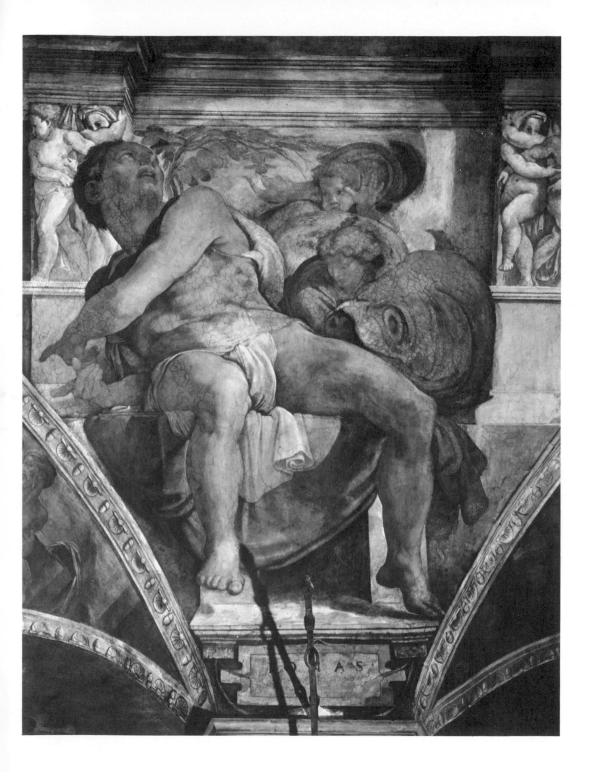

PLATE 18

The New Sacristy or Medici Chapel

Florence, S. Lorenzo

Michelangelo made in the sacristy four tombs to hold the bodies of the fathers of the two Popes: namely, the elder Lorenzo and his brother Giuliano, and those of Giuliano, the brother of Leo, and of Duke Lorenzo, Leo's nephew. He wanted to execute the work in imitation of the old sacristy made by Filippo Brunelleschi but with different decorative features; and so he did the ornamentation in a composite order, in a style more varied and more original than any other master, ancient or modern, has ever been able to achieve. For the beautiful cornices, capitals, bases, doors, tabernacles, and tombs were extremely novel, and in them he departed a great deal from the kind of architecture regulated by proportion, order, and rule which other artists did according to common usage and following Vitruvius and the works of antiquity but from which Michelangelo wanted to break away. (pp. 58–9)

The chapel was begun in 1520 and is one of the major works of Mannerist architecture, in accordance with Michelangelo's aims as stated by Vasari.

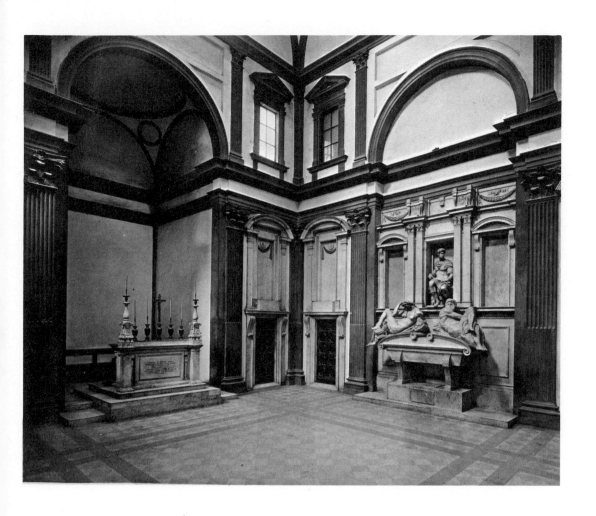

PLATE 19

Night, from the Tomb of Giuliano de' Medici

Marble, Florence, San Lorenzo

Meanwhile, he continued the work in . . . San Lorenzo, in which there were seven statues which were left partly finished and partly not. . . . So to one tomb he gave Night and Day, and to the other Dawn and Evening; and these statues are so beautifully formed, their attitudes so lovely, and their muscles treated so skilfully, that if the art of sculpture were lost they would serve to restore to it its original lustre. (pp. 60–1)

Many years later, Michelangelo wrote a poem on this statue, expressing his revulsion from the Medici tyranny which had succeeded the rule of the Medici who had been his early patrons. Giovanni Strozzi had written an epigram on the figure of Night, rather tritely suggesting that the stone figure 'carved by an Angel' would speak if one were to wake her from her sleep. Michelangelo replied in a four-line poem, in which Night speaks: 'Dear to me is sleep, and dearer to be of stone while wrongdoing and shame prevail; not to see, not to hear, is a great blessing: so do not awaken me; speak softly'.

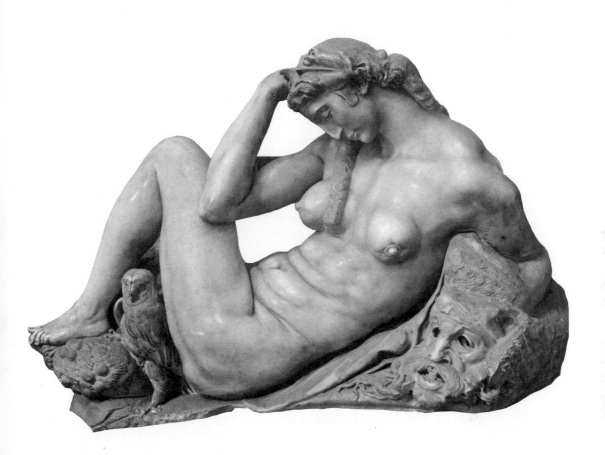

PLATE 20

The vestibule and stairs of the Biblioteca Laurenziana

Florence, San Lorenzo

Later Michelangelo sought to make known and to demonstrate his new ideas to even better effect in the library of San Lorenzo: namely, in the beautiful distribution of the windows, the pattern of the ceiling and the marvellous entrance of the vestibule. . . . And in this stairway, he made such strange breaks in the design of the steps, and he departed in so many details and so widely from normal practice, that everyone was astonished. (p. 59)

Vasari was then instructed by Duke Cosimo to write to Michelangelo asking him to reply saying what final form the stairway should have, in the hope that because of his love and friendship for Vasari he would say something that might lead to a solution and to the completion of the work. . . . So Michelangelo then sent the directions for making the stairway in a letter dated 28 September 1555.

Giorgio, my dear friend,

Concerning the stairway for the library that I've been asked about so much, believe me if I could remember how I planned it I would not need to be asked . . . (p. 95)

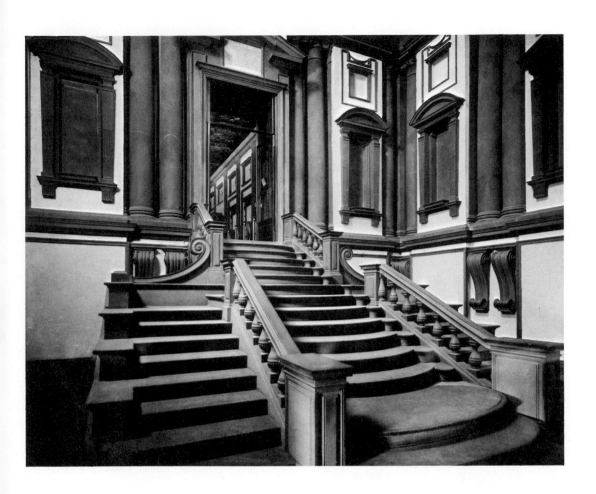

PLATE 21

The Risen Christ

Marble, Rome, Santa Maria sopra Minerva

It was at that time that Michelangelo sent his assistant, Pietro Urbino of Pistoia, to Rome to carry to completion a very fine figure of the naked Christ bearing the cross, which was placed on behalf of Antonio Metelli beside the principal chapel of Santa Maria sopra Minerva. Soon afterwards there took place the Sack of Rome . . . (pp. 59–60)

The dates implied in the quotation—about 1524 for the library at San Lorenzo, and before the Sack of Rome, which took place in 1527—make it seem that Michelangelo must have carved it then, but we know that the original contract dated from as early as 1514, although the first version was spoiled by an unexpected vein in the marble. The second version, worked on by Pietro Urbino (or Urbano) and much criticized by Sebastiano del Piombo in a letter to Michelangelo, was unveiled in December 1521.

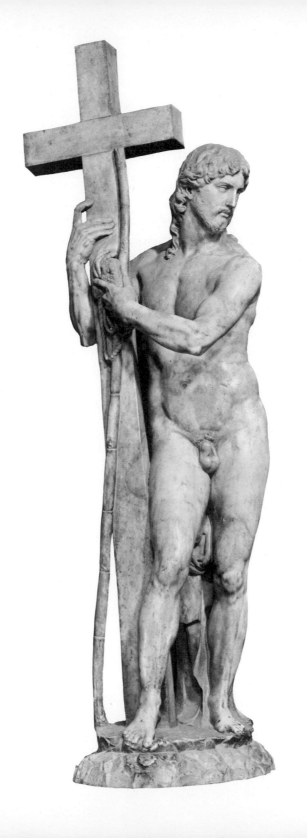

PLATE 22

Minos, detail from the Last Judgement

Fresco, Rome, Vatican

Michelangelo had already finished more than three-fourths of the work when Pope Paul went to see it. On this occasion Biagio da Cesena, the master of ceremonies and a very scrupulous person, happened to be with the Pope in the chapel and was asked what he thought of the painting. He answered that it was most disgraceful that in so sacred a place there should have been depicted all those nude figures, exposing themselves so shamefully, and that it was no work for a papal chapel but rather for the public baths and taverns. Angered by this comment, Michelangelo determined he would have his revenge; and as soon as Biagio had left he drew his portrait from memory in the figure of Minos, shown with a great serpent curled round his legs, among a heap of devils in hell; nor for all his pleading with the Pope and Michelangelo could Biagio have the figure removed, and it was left, to record the incident, as it is today. (p. 73)

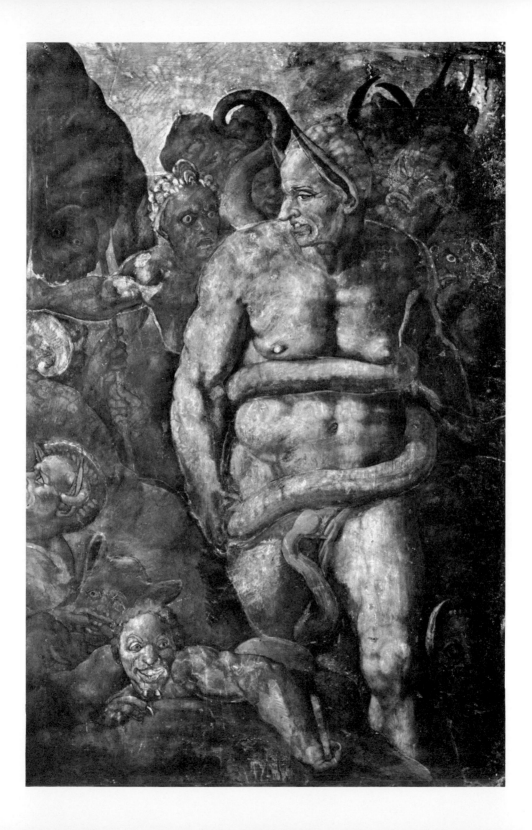

PLATE 23

Michelangelo, detail from The Crucifixion of St Peter

Fresco, Vatican, Cappella Paolina

Pope Paul had caused a chapel called the Pauline to be built . . . and for this he decided that Michelangelo should paint two large pictures. . . . These scenes, which he painted at the age of seventy-five, were the last pictures he did; and they cost him a great deal of effort, because painting, especially in fresco, is no work for men who have passed a certain age. (pp. 77–8)

The Pauline Chapel was painted between 1542 and 1550 (when, as Vasari says, Michelangelo was 75). This was the time of the Council of Trent and the Counter-Reform and Michelangelo himself was profoundly affected by the new spirituality. The self-portrait as a witness of the martyrdom is a reflection of this attitude.

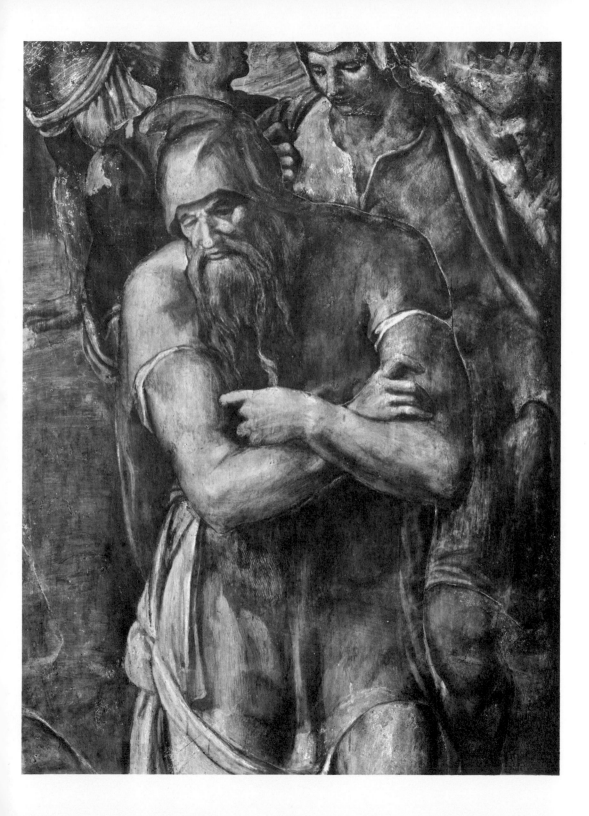

PLATE 24

Pietà

Marble, Florence, Cathedral

. . . since he was unable to paint, he set to work on a piece of marble, intending to carve four figures in the round and larger than life-size (including a dead Christ) to amuse and occupy himself and also, as he used to say himself, because using the hammer kept his body healthy. . . . Nowhere else can one see a dead form to compare with this figure of Christ; he is shown sinking down with his limbs hanging limp and he lies in an attitude altogether different not only from that of any other of Michelangelo's figures but from that of any other figure ever made. This work, the fruit of intense labour, was a rare achievement in a single stone and truly inspired; but, as will be told later on, it remained unfinished and suffered many misfortunes, although Michelangelo had intended it to go at the foot of the altar where he hoped to place his own tomb. (p. 79)

Michelangelo used to work every day, for recreation, on the block of stone with four figures that we have already mentioned; and at this time he broke it into pieces. He did this either because it was hard and full of emery and the chisel often struck sparks from it, or perhaps because his judgement was so severe that he was never content with anything he did . . . he gave the broken Pietà to Francesco Bandini. . . . It was immediately carried off and subsequently put together by Tiberio [Calcagni] who added God knows how many new pieces. (pp. 99–100)

Both this and the Rondanini Pietà *remained unfinished and fragmentary (cf. Plate 28), but, as Vasari says, they show Michelangelo inventing a new solution to the formal problems of the Pietà group, quite different from his St. Peter's one, and more in keeping with Counter-Reformation piety.*

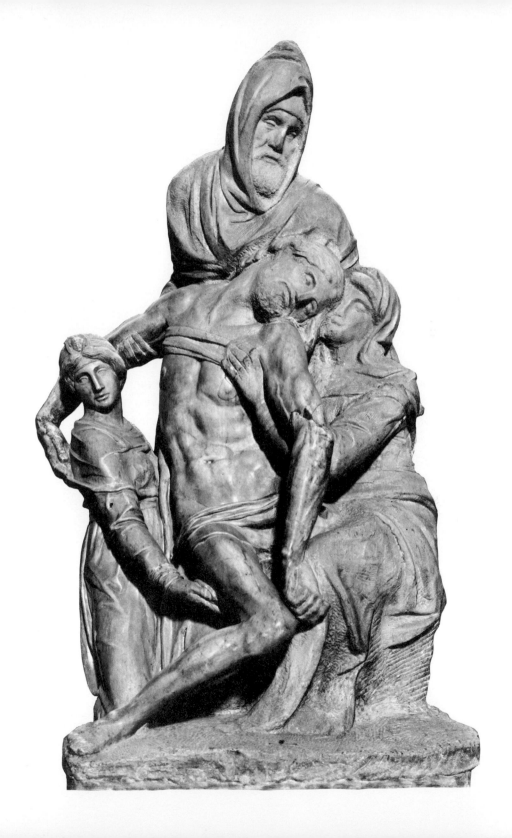

PLATE 25

Exterior of the apse of St Peter's, Rome

It happened that in 1546 Antonio da Sangallo died; and since there was now no one supervising the building of St. Peter's various suggestions were made by the superintendents to the Pope as to who should take over. At length (inspired I feel sure by God) his holiness resolved to send for Michelangelo. . . . The Pope eventually gave his approval to the model Michelangelo had made. This diminished the size of St. Peter's but increased its grandeur in a manner which pleases all those able to judge . . . (pp. 79–81)

Michelangelo was officially appointed to supervise St. Peter's on 1 January 1547 and held the post until his death in 1564. During these 17 years great progress was made, and the top of the drum was reached by 1564. Subsequent alterations, however, mean that very little of Michelangelo's building is now visible, and the back of the choir—which is not normally accessible to the ordinary tourist—is perhaps the best part from which to judge Michelangelo's late architectural style.

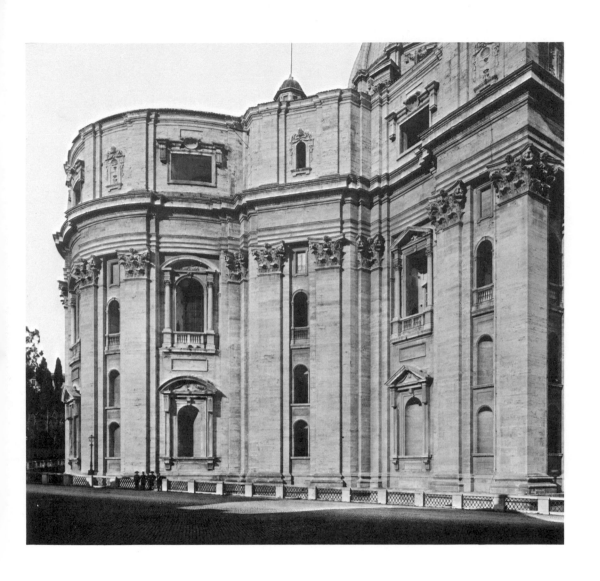

PLATE 26

Michelangelo's project for The Capitol, Rome

Engraving by Dupérac, London, Victoria and Albert Museum

The people of Rome, with the consent of Pope Paul, were anxious to give some useful, commodious, and beautiful form to the Capitol. . . . Michelangelo made for them a very rich and beautiful design. (p. 82)

This engraving by Dupérac was made in 1569, after Michelangelo's death, but it represents his original intentions. As executed, largely by Giacomo della Porta, important changes were made which have the effect of spoiling the unity of the conception.

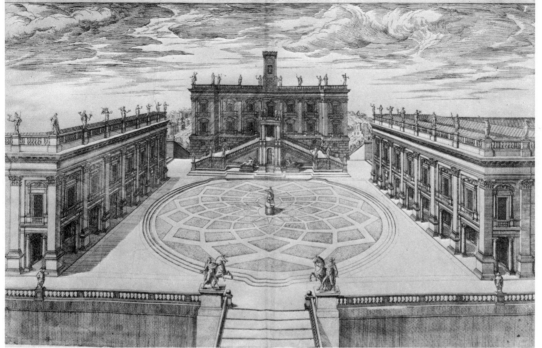

CAPITOLII·SCIOGRAPHIA·EX·IPSO·EXEMPLARI·MICHAELIS·ANGELI·BONAROTI·A·STEPHANO·DVPERAC·PARISIENSI·ACCVRATE·DELINEATA
ET·IN·LVCEM·AEDITA·ROMAE·ANNO·SALVTIS·∞ᴅLXIX

PLATE 27

Detail of a window in the court of the
Palazzo Farnese, Rome

Consequently, after Sangallo died, the Pope wanted Michelangelo to take charge of the whole building as well; and so Michelangelo made the great marble window . . . above the principal door of the palace. . . . Within the palace over the first storey of the courtyard Michelangelo continued the two other storeys, with their incomparably beautiful, graceful, and varied windows, ornamentation and crowning cornice. (pp. 83–4)

The design of the Farnese Palace is contemporary with the first projects for St. Peter's (cf. Plate 25) and the very free handling of classical detail is characteristic of Michelangelo's last style, to be so influential on the architects of Baroque Rome.

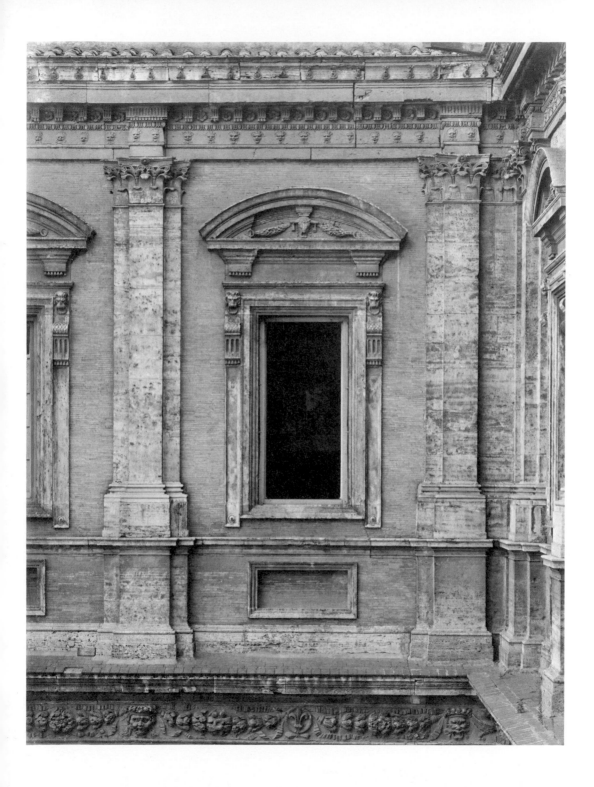

PLATE 28

The Rondanini Pietà

Marble statue, Milan, Civico Museo Sforzesco

To return to Michelangelo: it was now necessary for him to find another block of marble, so that he could continue using his chisel every day; so he found a far smaller block [than the one used for the *Pietà* in Plate 24] containing a Pietà already roughed out and of a very different arrangement. (p. 101)

This was Michelangelo's last work, on which he was still engaged a few days before his death. The theme of the Pietà is treated as a personal meditation and the abstract quality of the forms proves that he can never have intended to 'finish' it for public exhibition. Vasari's remark that the block already contained an earlier version of the subject is borne out by the presence of a second right arm of the figure of Christ and another version of the head of the Virgin. Vasari continues his account by saying that, at this time, Michelangelo was preoccupied with thoughts of death and wrote the sonnet Giunto è gia'l corso della vita mia *(translated on p. 102).*

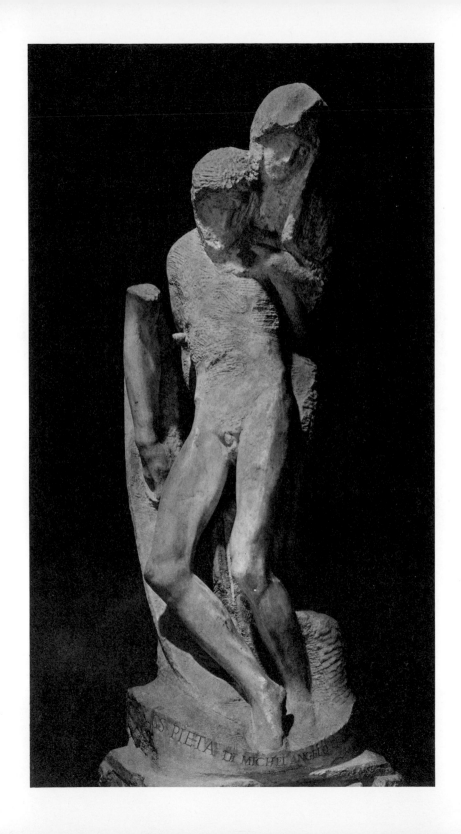

PLATE 29

Andrea Quaratesi

Black chalk, London, British Museum

Michelangelo did a portrait of Tommaso [de' Cavalieri] in a life-size cartoon, but neither before nor afterwards did he do any other portrait from life, because he hated drawing any living subject unless it were of exceptional beauty. (p. 123)

In spite of Vasari's explicit statement, this drawing may well be by Michelangelo and date from about 1532. The late Johannes Wilde attributed it to Michelangelo, pointing out that there is a seventeenth-century copy in the Uffizi which has an inscription by the sitter's grandson, dated 1645, in which he not only identifies Andrea, but also says that the original was by Michelangelo.

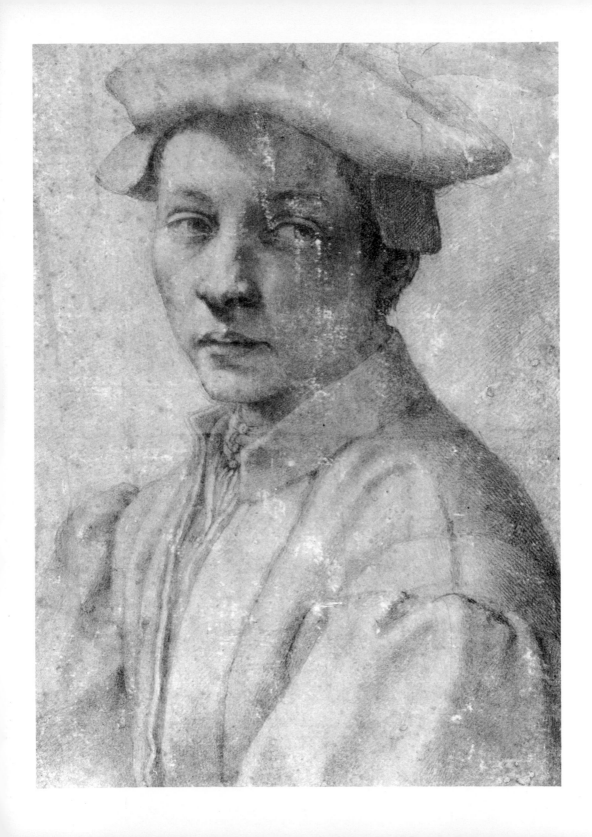

PLATE 30

Christ on the Cross

Black chalk, London, British Museum

Michelangelo sent any number of his verses to the Marchioness of Pescara, who replied to him in both verse and prose. . . . For her, Michelangelo designed a Pietà. . . . As well as this admirable work he did an inspired Christ nailed to the cross, with his head uplifted and commending his spirit to the Father . . . (p. 125)

This is almost certainly the drawing referred to by Vasari (who took the information from Michelangelo's earlier biographer, Condivi). It must have been drawn about 1541.

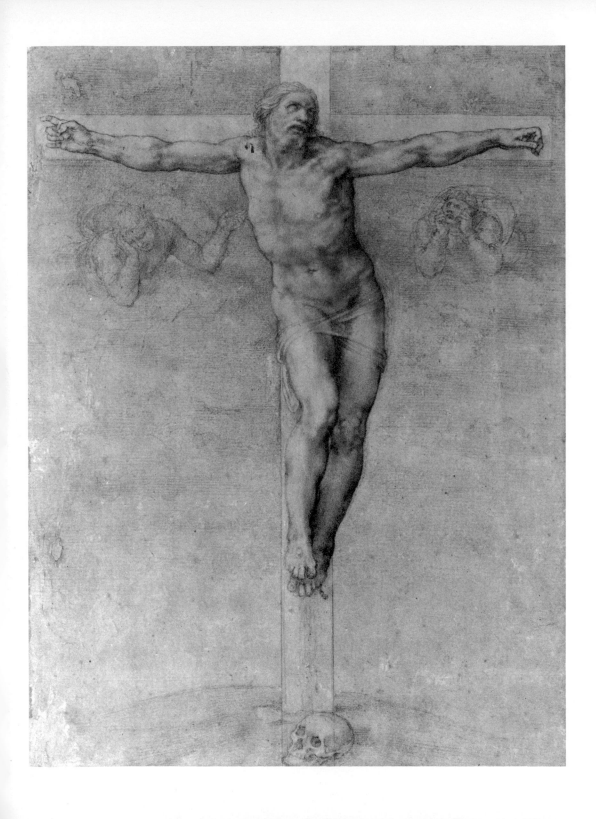

PLATE 31

A Captive

Unfinished marble statue, Florence, Accademia

. . . and four other captives in the rough which serve to teach us how
to carve figures out of marble by a method which leaves no chance of
spoiling the stone. This method is as follows: one must take a figure
of wax or some other firm material and lay it horizontally in a vessel
of water; then, as the water is, of course, flat and level, when the figure
is raised little by little above the surface the more salient parts are
revealed first, while the lower parts (on the underside of the figure)
remain submerged, until eventually it all comes into view. In the same
way figures must be carved out of marble by the chisel; the parts in
highest relief must be revealed first and then little by little the lower
parts. And this method can be seen to have been followed by Michelangelo in the statues of the prisoners . . . (pp. 123–4)